THIS BOOK BELONGS TO

_____

START DATE

_____

SHE READS TRUTH

EXECUTIVE

FOUNDER/CHIEF EXECUTIVE OFFICER
Raechel Myers

CO-FOUNDER/CHIEF CONTENT OFFICER
Amanda Bible Williams

CHIEF OPERATING OFFICER
Ryan Myers

EDITORIAL

CONTENT DIRECTOR
Jessica Lamb

DIGITAL MANAGING EDITOR
Oghosa Iyamu, MDiv

PRODUCTION EDITOR
Hannah Little, MTS

MARKETING CONTENT EDITOR
Tameshia Williams, ThM

ASSOCIATE EDITOR
Lindsey Jacobi, MDiv

OPERATIONS

OPERATIONS DIRECTOR
Allison Sutton

OFFICE MANAGER
Nicole Quirion

PROJECT ASSISTANT
Mary Beth Montgomery

CREATIVE

CREATIVE DIRECTOR
Amy Dennis

DESIGN MANAGER
Kelsea Allen

ART DIRECTOR
Aimee Lindamood

DESIGNERS
Abbey Benson
Amanda Brush, MA
Annie Glover
Lauren Haag

JUNIOR DESIGNER
Jessie Gerakinis

MARKETING

MARKETING DIRECTOR
Kamron Kunce

GROWTH MARKETING MANAGER
Blake Showalter

PRODUCT MARKETING MANAGER
Megan Phillips

SOCIAL MEDIA STRATEGIST
Taylor Krupp

SHIPPING

SHIPPING MANAGER
Marian Byne

FULFILLMENT LEAD
Cait Baggerman

FULFILLMENT SPECIALISTS
Kajsa Matheny
Noe Sanchez

SUBSCRIPTION INQUIRIES
orders@shereadstruth.com

COMMUNITY SUPPORT

COMMUNITY EXPERIENCE DIRECTOR
Kara Hewett, MOL

COMMUNITY SUPPORT SPECIALISTS
Katy McKnight
Heather Vollono
Margot Williams

CONTRIBUTORS

RECIPES
Margaret Feinberg (46, 104)

SPECIAL THANKS
Beth Joseph
Sugar Drop Bakery

 @SHEREADSTRUTH

Download the She Reads Truth app, available for iOS and Android

 Subscribe to the She Reads Truth podcast

SHEREADSTRUTH.COM

YOUR PEOPLE FOREVER

A LENTEN STUDY OF 1 & 2 CHRONICLES

The promise of God's
restoration after rebellion
is our story as well.

Jessica Lamb
CONTENT DIRECTOR

"Who reads Chronicles?" I laughed when I opened an Old Testament reference book and found these words inauspiciously beginning the chapter on 1 & 2 Chronicles. It's probably safe to assume some of you wondered the same thing. For those of us more familiar with the words of Paul, James, John, and Luke, the genealogies, kings, and construction details found in Chronicles can be over (or even under) whelming.

Though 1 & 2 Chronicles may be stylistically different from the narratives and letters of the New Testament, they were written to answer questions we still ask today. *How do I trust God after my life has gone so much differently than I expected? How do we live rightly as the people of God here and now? How do we trust that Christ will come, thousands of years after we were promised He would?*

As you'll read in the introduction on pages 15–20, Chronicles was written as the Israelites returned from exile. The author looked back over generations to encourage the Israelites that there was life to be found on the other side of exile. Our circumstances are different, but the promise of God's restoration after rebellion is our story as well, one both Chronicles and the Lenten season help us to remember.

In the genealogies that span the first several chapters of Chronicles, we experience how our individual lives are brought into the larger, ongoing story of God's family legacy (pages 22–45). The details of the temple demonstrate how sacrifice and renewal are a starting place for an intimate encounter with God's presence (pages 52–121). When a king's decades-long reign is summarized in a handful of verses, we begin to understand how futile it is to put all our hopes in the tenure of an earthly leader over investing in God's kingdom (pages 128–201).

We learn through these books to look back at the faithfulness of God when we don't know how to move forward. Covering over 2,000 years of God's people waiting through highs and lows for a perfect King and kingdom, these books model how to turn and return to God as we wait in anticipation for Christ's return almost 2,000 years after His resurrection and ascension.

As we read Chronicles this Lent, our hope isn't that we walk away having memorized every detail in the temple or lists of lineage. It's that we arrive at Holy Week changed by the Word, celebrating at Easter the legacy and longevity of our God, our salvation, and the eternal hope we are offered in Christ.

At She Reads Truth, we believe in pairing the inherently beautiful Word of God with the aesthetic beauty it deserves. Each of our resources is thoughtfully and artfully designed to highlight the beauty, goodness, and truth of Scripture in a way that reflects the themes of each curated reading plan.

The design of this book is centered around the custom clay art pieces featured throughout. The photos show our artist molding and draping the clay. Both the process and the product reflect the book of Chronicles. The meditative and tactile nature of the artistic process helps us to remember God's faithfulness in the past and the highs and lows reflected in the story of God's people. The final piece of art itself is a token of remembrance pointing us to the finished work of Christ that we anticipate during Lent and celebrate at Easter.

HOW TO USE THIS BOOK

She Reads Truth is a community of women dedicated to reading the Word of God every day. In this Lenten season we will spend six weeks in the books of 1 & 2 Chronicles, reflecting on the historical, unwavering faithfulness of God toward His people. Then, we will spend Holy Week primarily in the Gospel of John as we journey from Palm Sunday to Easter Sunday.

READ & REFLECT

The **Your People Forever: A Lenten Study of 1 & 2 Chronicles** Study Book focuses primarily on Scripture, with added features to come alongside your time with God's Word.

SCRIPTURE READING

Designed for a Monday start, this Study Book presents the books of 1 & 2 Chronicles in daily readings, along with additional passages curated to show how themes from the main reading can be found throughout Scripture. The last week of reading focuses on Holy Week.

 Additional passages are marked in your daily reading with the Going Deeper heading.

RESPONSE

Each weekday features space for notes, along with three extended moments of reflection.

COMMUNITY & CONVERSATION

From Raleigh to Romania, the She Reads Truth community will start Day 1 of Lent 2023 on Monday, February 20, 2023.

SHE READS TRUTH APP

Devotionals corresponding to each daily reading can be found in the **Lent 2023: Your People Forever** reading plan on the She Reads Truth app. New devotionals will be published each weekday once the plan begins on Monday, February 20, 2023. You can use the app to participate in community discussion and more.

GRACE DAY

Use Saturdays to catch up on your reading, pray, and rest in the presence of the Lord.

WEEKLY TRUTH

Sundays are set aside for Scripture memorization.

See tips for memorizing Scripture on page 240.

EXTRAS

This book features additional tools to help you gain a deeper understanding of the text.

Find a complete list of extras on page 13.

 SHEREADSTRUTH.COM

This reading plan, along with devotionals, will also be available at SheReadsTruth.com as the community reads each day. Invite your family, friends, and neighbors to read along with you!

 SHE READS TRUTH PODCAST

Subscribe to the She Reads Truth podcast and join our founders and their guests each week as they talk about what you'll read in the week ahead.

 Podcast episodes *168–174* for our **Lent 2023: Your People Forever** series release on Mondays beginning February 20, 2023.

Table of Contents

THE LINEAGE OF GOD'S PEOPLE

> **WEEK 01**

DAY 1	From Adam to Abraham	24
DAY 2	The Genealogies of Judah and David	28
DAY 3	The Genealogy of the Levites	34
DAY 4	The Genealogies of the Northern and Central Tribes	38
DAY 5	Resettlement in Jerusalem	42
DAY 6	Grace Day	48
DAY 7	Weekly Truth	50

GOD'S PEOPLE UNITED

> **WEEK 02**

DAY 8	David's Anointing as King	54
DAY 9	David Moves the Ark of the Covenant	60
DAY 10	David Gives Thanks to the Lord	66
DAY 11	The Lord's Covenant with David	70
DAY 12	David's Military Campaigns	74
DAY 13	Grace Day	80
DAY 14	Weekly Truth	82

GOD'S PEOPLE UNITED

WEEK 03

DAY 15	Preparations for the Temple	84
DAY 16	The Divisions of the Levites	88
DAY 17	The Levitical Gatekeepers	92
DAY 18	David Commissions Solomon	96
DAY 19	Solomon's Request for Wisdom	100
DAY 20	Grace Day	106
DAY 21	Weekly Truth	108

WEEK 04

DAY 22	Building the Temple	110
DAY 23	The Dedication of the Temple	116
DAY 24	The Queen of Sheba Seeks Solomon's Wisdom	124
DAY 25	Rehoboam Abandons God's Law	130
DAY 26	Revival Under King Asa	134
DAY 27	Grace Day	140
DAY 28	Weekly Truth	142

GOD'S PEOPLE DIVIDED

GOD'S PEOPLE DIVIDED

WEEK 05

DAY 29	Judah's King Jehoshaphat	144
DAY 30	King Jehoshaphat's Reforms	148
DAY 31	King Jehoram Leads Judah Astray	154
DAY 32	King Joash's Apostasy	158
DAY 33	King Amaziah Turns from the Lord	162
DAY 34	Grace Day	168
DAY 35	Weekly Truth	170

WEEK 06

DAY 36	King Ahaz's Unfaithfulness	172
DAY 37	Renewal Under King Hezekiah	176
DAY 38	Manasseh's Repentance	186
DAY 39	King Josiah Renews the Covenant	192
DAY 40	The Last Kings of Judah	198
DAY 41	Grace Day	204

HOLY WEEK

WEEK 07

DAY 42	Palm Sunday	210
DAY 43	Jesus Washes His Disciples' Feet	214
DAY 44	Jesus Promises His Presence	218
DAY 45	The Promised Counselor	222
DAY 46	Jesus Prays for His Disciples	226
DAY 47	Good Friday	230
DAY 48	Holy Saturday	234
DAY 49	Easter Sunday	236

EXTRAS

She Reads 1 & 2 Chronicles	16
What Is Lent?	18
Why 1 & 2 Chronicles for Lent?	20
RECIPE: Roasted Figs and Brussels Sprouts	46
Israel and Judah	64
HYMN: Crown Him with Many Crowns	78
RECIPE: Chocolate Pomegranate Drops	104
Solomon's Temple	114
Response: Repent	122
HYMN: Come, Thou Fount of Every Blessing	166
Christ as Prophet, Priest, and King	182
Response: Reflect	202
Response: Prepare	208
For the Record	244

KEY PASSAGES

Yours, Lord, is the greatness and the power and the glory and the splendor and the majesty, for everything in the heavens and on earth belongs to you. Yours, Lord, is the kingdom, and you are exalted as head over all.

1 CHRONICLES 29:11

"If I shut the sky so there is no rain, or if I command the grasshopper to consume the land, or if I send pestilence on my people, and my people, who bear my name, humble themselves, pray and seek my face, and turn from their evil ways, then I will hear from heaven, forgive their sin, and heal their land."

2 CHRONICLES 7:13–14

She Reads 1 & 2 Chronicles

ON THE TIMELINE

Like 1 & 2 Kings, 1 & 2 Chronicles may have originally been one work, the book of Chronicles. The book of Kings was written to an audience currently living in exile, while Chronicles was written sometime after the return from the exile, perhaps the middle of the fifth century BC. These different accounts of the same history were written to two separate audiences that needed their own unique messages.

The book of 1 Chronicles includes extensive genealogies beginning with Adam, focusing on the reign of King David. After the genealogies, the events in 1 Chronicles begin with the deaths of Saul and his sons and King David's rise to the throne in Israel, around 1010 BC. The book concludes with the death of King David and the enthronement of Solomon in 970 BC.

The book of 2 Chronicles focuses on the kings after David through the exile and reinstatement of Jerusalem (970 BC to 538 BC). It records the same time period as 1 & 2 Kings, but 2 Chronicles focuses primarily on the kings of Judah and carries a more restorative and hopeful tone.

A LITTLE BACKGROUND

First and 2 Chronicles are the first and second books of a four-book series that includes Ezra and Nehemiah. Together, these four books provide a priestly history of Israel from the time of Adam to the rebuilding of the house of God and the walls of Jerusalem. It is likely that 1 & 2 Chronicles were, at one time, a single scroll.

An ancient tradition suggests the author of Chronicles (often known as the Chronicler) was Ezra. Among other criteria, this identification is supported by the fact that the last verses of Chronicles are the first verses of the book of Ezra. In the Christian canon, Ezra and Nehemiah immediately follow 1 & 2 Chronicles, continuing to tell the story of Israel's return from exile.

MESSAGE & PURPOSE

Having resettled in Jerusalem after the exile, the Israelites needed to reconnect with their identity as the people of God. Chronicles met this purpose by reminding them of their heritage and by directing them back to God's presence in their midst as symbolized by the temple.

Important ideas emphasized in 1 & 2 Chronicles are:

① A direct connection to God's people in the past

② The continuity of the line of David on the throne of Judah

③ The importance of the priestly lineage of the Levites

④ The centrality of the temple and worship according to God's instruction

⑤ The favor God's people experience when they obey His covenant

⑥ The consequences God's people face when they disobey His covenant

GIVE THANKS FOR THE BOOKS OF 1 & 2 CHRONICLES

Chronicles brings together many dimensions of biblical revelation, such as historical events (as recounted in Genesis through 2 Kings), temple ritual (as prescribed in Leviticus), sin and judgment (as preached by the prophets), and even some psalms. The books of 1 & 2 Chronicles give us the big picture of Old Testament history, capturing the Davidic covenant in light of Israel's history back to Adam and pointing to the eternal continuation of that covenant through the reign of the Messiah.

What Is Lent?

For more than a thousand years, Christians around the world have observed Lent as a solemn season of self-reflection, repentance, and Scripture meditation as a means of preparing to celebrate Easter. As contemporary believers, we are invited—though not required—to do the same.

LENT AS REMEMBRANCE

God formed us from the dust of the earth, declared us to be good, and gave us the honor of bearing His image (Gn 1:27).

But the first humans rebelled against God (Gn 3:1–7). And generations later, we continue to turn away from Him. Because of this, our relationships with God, one another, and all of creation are subject to the death, decay, and frustration that comes from sin (Rm 8:20–21).

The redemptive story of Scripture culminates in God coming to earth to meet our need. Jesus Christ, God the Son, came to deliver us and restore peace and order through His life, death, and resurrection (Jn 3:16–17; Rm 5:1–2). Through faith, we are forgiven of our sins and brought into a saving relationship with God for eternity (Rm 10:11–13; Eph 2:8–9).

Through the gift of the Holy Spirit, we are actively being made into the image of Christ. We are also invited to play a role in God's redemptive work in the world as we await the day all creation will be perfectly restored.

During Lent, we reflect on this greater redemption narrative where we are met face-to-face with our desperate need for salvation. In this long, slow season, we remember our need for forgiveness in order to truly rejoice in the unmatched, indescribable way our loving and merciful God meets that need.

LENT AND THE CHURCH CALENDAR

The season of Lent is just one part of the Church calendar, a centuries-old way many Christian denominations order the year to remember and celebrate the redeeming work of Christ.

Structured around the moving date of Easter Sunday and the fixed date of Christmas, the liturgical Church calendar consists of six seasons as well as ordinary time. Listed here are the three seasons related to Jesus's ministry of reconciliation on earth, as well as the arrival of the Holy Spirit.

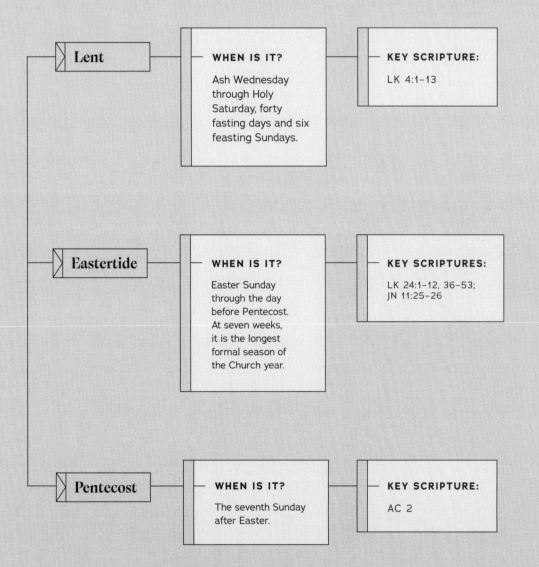

Lent

WHEN IS IT?

Ash Wednesday through Holy Saturday, forty fasting days and six feasting Sundays.

KEY SCRIPTURE:

LK 4:1–13

Eastertide

WHEN IS IT?

Easter Sunday through the day before Pentecost. At seven weeks, it is the longest formal season of the Church year.

KEY SCRIPTURES:

LK 24:1–12, 36–53; JN 11:25–26

Pentecost

WHEN IS IT?

The seventh Sunday after Easter.

KEY SCRIPTURE:

AC 2

Why 1 & 2 Chronicles for Lent?

The books of 1 & 2 Chronicles are a condensed account of Israel's history. Together, they demonstrate that God is faithful to His promises at every turn—from the creation of Adam, through the call of Abraham and the forming of Israel, all the way to the return of God's people from exile.

After seventy years in Babylonian exile, the Israelites had returned to their home. But their years in exile left them doubtful and disheartened, questioning their place in history and God's authority and power. *Did they still have a future as God's people? What would they do now? How would they start over?*

During this pivotal return, the author of Chronicles wrote to encourage the Israelite people to look back to the very beginning of their story with God to see His presence at every point of their journey. God was still the author of this story. His promises were still true. He called the Israelite people then, and He still had a plan for their future.

Chronicles is not just lengthy genealogies and historical accounts. Chronicles still acts as an anchor point for the people of God today, because we too are prone to forget. As followers of Jesus, we sometimes lose sight of the new life that was won for us at the cross and the empty tomb.

The season of Lent invites us to look back and reflect on the whole story of redemption. We can remember and acknowledge our propensity toward sin and our desperate state apart from Christ. We can repent for the many ways we have tried in vain to rescue ourselves. And we can proclaim God's promises that have always been true. Through Chronicles, we encounter Lent as an invitation to reorient our lives toward right relationship and right worship of the one true God.

Chronicles ends with redemption and the hope of a new beginning after exile. Having looked back, God's people can move forward, walking in restoration. That's how the season of Lent ends, as Easter Sunday dawns with the hope of new life because Christ has conquered death. We remember in this story who has made a way. We repent where we have turned away. And we celebrate the resurrection with the assurance that God's promises are still true. King Jesus has come, and He sits on the throne forever.

The Lineage of God's People

1 CHRONICLES 1–9

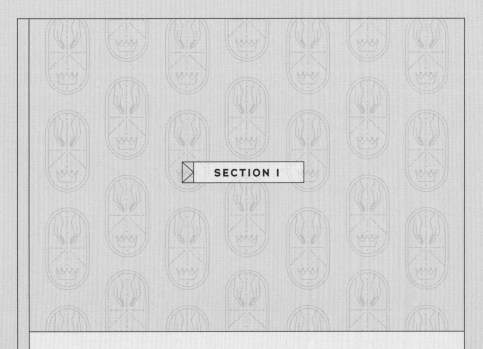

SECTION I

First Chronicles opens with nine chapters of genealogies, setting the stage for everything the Chronicler is attempting to record for the people of Israel. Starting with creation, the author traces the family lines from Adam to Abraham, each of the twelve tribes of Israel, and on through the reign of King David. The Chronicler gives special attention to the family lines of Judah, from whom David descended, and the priestly lineage of the Levites.

These chapters pointed God's people, recently returned to Israel from seventy years in Babylonian exile, to the hope of the coming Messiah from Judah and David's line. They also point to the hope of restored worship according to God's instruction.

THE
LINEAGE
OF GOD'S
PEOPLE

From Adam to Abraham

1 CHRONICLES 1

From Adam to Abraham

¹ Adam, Seth, Enosh,

² Kenan, Mahalalel, Jared,

³ Enoch, Methuselah, Lamech,

⁴ Noah, Noah's sons:

Shem, Ham, and Japheth.

⁵ Japheth's sons: Gomer, Magog, Madai, Javan, Tubal, Meshech, and Tiras.

⁶ Gomer's sons: Ashkenaz, Riphath, and Togarmah.

⁷ Javan's sons: Elishah, Tarshish, Kittim, and Rodanim.

⁸ Ham's sons: Cush, Mizraim, Put, and Canaan.

⁹ Cush's sons: Seba, Havilah, Sabta, Raama, and Sabteca.

Raama's sons: Sheba and Dedan.

¹⁰ Cush fathered Nimrod, who was the first to become a great warrior on earth.

¹¹ Mizraim fathered the people of Lud, Anam, Lehab, Naphtuh, ¹² Pathrus, Casluh (the Philistines came from them), and Caphtor.

¹³ Canaan fathered Sidon as his firstborn and Heth, ¹⁴ as well as the Jebusites, Amorites, Girgashites, ¹⁵ Hivites, Arkites, Sinites, ¹⁶ Arvadites, Zemarites, and Hamathites.

¹⁷ Shem's sons: Elam, Asshur, Arpachshad, Lud, Aram, Uz, Hul, Gether, and Meshech.

¹⁸ Arpachshad fathered Shelah, and Shelah fathered Eber. ¹⁹ Two sons were born to Eber. One of them was named Peleg because the earth was divided during his lifetime, and the name of his brother was Joktan. ²⁰ Joktan fathered Almodad, Sheleph, Hazarmaveth, Jerah, ²¹ Hadoram, Uzal, Diklah, ²² Ebal, Abimael, Sheba, ²³ Ophir, Havilah, and Jobab. All of these were Joktan's sons.

²⁴ Shem, Arpachshad, Shelah,

²⁵ Eber, Peleg, Reu,

²⁶ Serug, Nahor, Terah,

²⁷ and Abram (that is, Abraham).

Abraham's Descendants

²⁸ Abraham's sons: Isaac and Ishmael.

²⁹ These are their family records: Nebaioth, Ishmael's firstborn, Kedar, Adbeel, Mibsam, ³⁰ Mishma, Dumah, Massa, Hadad, Tema, ³¹ Jetur, Naphish, and Kedemah.

These were Ishmael's sons.

³² The sons born to Keturah, Abraham's concubine: Zimran, Jokshan, Medan, Midian, Ishbak, and Shuah.

Jokshan's sons: Sheba and Dedan.

³³ Midian's sons: Ephah, Epher, Hanoch, Abida, and Eldaah.

All of these were Keturah's descendants.

³⁴ Abraham fathered Isaac.

Isaac's sons: Esau and Israel.

³⁵ Esau's sons: Eliphaz, Reuel, Jeush, Jalam, and Korah.

³⁶ Eliphaz's sons: Teman, Omar, Zephi, Gatam, and Kenaz; and by Timna, Amalek.

³⁷ Reuel's sons: Nahath, Zerah, Shammah, and Mizzah.

The Edomites

³⁸ Seir's sons: Lotan, Shobal, Zibeon, Anah, Dishon, Ezer, and Dishan.

³⁹ Lotan's sons: Hori and Homam. Timna was Lotan's sister.

⁴⁰ Shobal's sons: Alian, Manahath, Ebal, Shephi, and Onam.

Zibeon's sons: Aiah and Anah.

⁴¹ Anah's son: Dishon.

Dishon's sons: Hamran, Eshban, Ithran, and Cheran.

⁴² Ezer's sons: Bilhan, Zaavan, and Jaakan.

Dishan's sons: Uz and Aran.

⁴³ These were the kings who reigned in the land of Edom

before any king reigned over the Israelites:

Bela son of Beor.

Bela's town was named Dinhabah.

⁴⁴ When Bela died, Jobab son of Zerah from Bozrah reigned in his place.

⁴⁵ When Jobab died, Husham from the land of the Temanites reigned in his place.

⁴⁶ When Husham died, Hadad son of Bedad, who defeated Midian in the territory of Moab, reigned in his place.

Hadad's town was named Avith.

⁴⁷ When Hadad died, Samlah from Masrekah reigned in his place.

⁴⁸ When Samlah died, Shaul from Rehoboth on the Euphrates River reigned in his place.

⁴⁹ When Shaul died, Baal-hanan son of Achbor reigned in his place.

⁵⁰ When Baal-hanan died, Hadad reigned in his place.

Hadad's city was named Pai, and his wife's name was Mehetabel

daughter of Matred, daughter of Me-zahab.

⁵¹ Then Hadad died.

Edom's chiefs: Timna, Alvah, Jetheth, ⁵² Oholibamah, Elah, Pinon, ⁵³ Kenaz, Teman, Mibzar, ⁵⁴ Magdiel, and Iram.

These were Edom's chiefs.

■ GOING DEEPER

PSALM 119:90

Your faithfulness is for all generations;
you established the earth, and it stands firm.

GALATIANS 3:16

Now the promises were spoken to Abraham
and to his seed.

He does not say "and to seeds," as though referring to many, but referring to one, and to your seed, who is Christ.

THE
LINEAGE
OF GOD'S
PEOPLE

WEEK 1   DAY 2

The Genealogies of Judah and David

1 CHRONICLES 2

Israel's Sons

¹ These were Israel's sons:
Reuben, Simeon, Levi,
Judah, Issachar, Zebulun,
² Dan, Joseph, Benjamin,
Naphtali, Gad, and Asher.

Judah's Descendants

³ Judah's sons: Er, Onan, and Shelah. These three were born to him by Bath-shua the Canaanite woman. Er, Judah's firstborn, was evil in the LORD's sight, so he put him to death. ⁴ Judah's daughter-in-law Tamar bore Perez and Zerah to him. Judah had five sons in all.

⁵ Perez's sons: Hezron and Hamul.
⁶ Zerah's sons: Zimri, Ethan, Heman, Calcol, and Dara—five in all.
⁷ Carmi's son: Achar, who brought trouble on Israel when he was unfaithful by taking the things set apart for destruction.
⁸ Ethan's son: Azariah.
⁹ Hezron's sons, who were born to him: Jerahmeel, Ram, and Chelubai.
¹⁰ Ram fathered Amminadab, and Amminadab fathered Nahshon, a leader of Judah's descendants.

¹¹ Nahshon fathered Salma, and Salma fathered Boaz.

¹² Boaz fathered Obed, and Obed fathered Jesse.

¹³ Jesse fathered Eliab, his firstborn; Abinadab was born second, Shimea third, ¹⁴ Nethanel fourth, Raddai fifth, ¹⁵ Ozem sixth, and David seventh. ¹⁶ Their sisters were Zeruiah and Abigail. Zeruiah's three sons: Abishai, Joab, and Asahel. ¹⁷ Amasa's mother was Abigail, and his father was Jether the Ishmaelite.

¹⁸ Caleb son of Hezron had children by his wife Azubah and by Jerioth. These were Azubah's sons: Jesher, Shobab, and Ardon. ¹⁹ When Azubah died, Caleb married Ephrath, and she bore Hur to him. ²⁰ Hur fathered Uri, and Uri fathered Bezalel. ²¹ After this, Hezron slept with the daughter of Machir the father of Gilead. Hezron had married her when he was sixty years old, and she bore Segub to him. ²² Segub fathered Jair, who possessed twenty-three towns in the land of Gilead. ²³ But Geshur and Aram captured Jair's Villages along with Kenath and its surrounding villages—sixty towns. All these were the descendants of Machir father of Gilead. ²⁴ After Hezron's death in Caleb-ephrathah, his wife Abijah bore Ashhur to him. He was the father of Tekoa.

²⁵ The sons of Jerahmeel, Hezron's firstborn: Ram, his firstborn, Bunah, Oren, Ozem, and Ahijah. ²⁶ Jerahmeel had another wife named Atarah, who was the mother of Onam.

²⁷ The sons of Ram, Jerahmeel's firstborn: Maaz, Jamin, and Eker.

²⁸ Onam's sons: Shammai and Jada.

Shammai's sons: Nadab and Abishur. ²⁹ Abishur's wife was named Abihail, who bore Ahban and Molid to him.

³⁰ Nadab's sons: Seled and Appaim. Seled died without children.

³¹ Appaim's son: Ishi.

Ishi's son: Sheshan.

Sheshan's descendant: Ahlai.

³² The sons of Jada, brother of Shammai: Jether and Jonathan. Jether died without children.

³³ Jonathan's sons: Peleth and Zaza. These were the descendants of Jerahmeel.

³⁴ Sheshan had no sons, only daughters, but he did have an Egyptian servant whose name was Jarha. ³⁵ Sheshan gave his daughter in marriage to his servant Jarha, and she bore Attai to him.

³⁶ Attai fathered Nathan, and Nathan fathered Zabad.

³⁷ Zabad fathered Ephlal, and Ephlal fathered Obed.

³⁸ Obed fathered Jehu, and Jehu fathered Azariah.

³⁹ Azariah fathered Helez, and Helez fathered Elasah.

⁴⁰ Elasah fathered Sismai, and Sismai fathered Shallum.

⁴¹ Shallum fathered Jekamiah, and Jekamiah fathered Elishama.

⁴² The sons of Caleb brother of Jerahmeel: Mesha, his firstborn, fathered Ziph, and Mareshah, his second son, fathered Hebron.

⁴³ Hebron's sons: Korah, Tappuah, Rekem, and Shema.

⁴⁴ Shema fathered Raham, who fathered Jorkeam, and Rekem fathered Shammai.

⁴⁵ Shammai's son was Maon, and Maon fathered Beth-zur.

⁴⁶ Caleb's concubine Ephah was the mother of Haran, Moza, and Gazez. Haran fathered Gazez.

⁴⁷ Jahdai's sons: Regem, Jotham, Geshan, Pelet, Ephah, and Shaaph.

⁴⁸ Caleb's concubine Maacah was the mother of Sheber and Tirhanah. ⁴⁹ She was also the mother of Shaaph, Madmannah's father, and of Sheva, the father of Machbenah and Gibea. Caleb's daughter was Achsah.

⁵⁰ These were Caleb's descendants.

The sons of Hur, Ephrathah's firstborn:

Shobal fathered Kiriath-jearim;

⁵¹ Salma fathered Bethlehem,

and Hareph fathered Beth-gader.

⁵² These were the descendants of Shobal the father of Kiriath-jearim: Haroeh, half of the Manahathites, ⁵³ and the families of Kiriath-jearim—the Ithrites, Puthites, Shumathites, and Mishraites. The Zorathites and Eshtaolites descended from these.

⁵⁴ Salma's descendants: Bethlehem, the Netophathites, Atroth-beth-joab, and half of the Manahathites, the Zorites, ⁵⁵ and the families of scribes who lived in Jabez—the Tirathites, Shimeathites, and Sucathites. These are the Kenites who came from Hammath, the father of Rechab's family.

1 CHRONICLES 3

David's Descendants

[1] These were David's sons who were born to him in Hebron:

Amnon was the firstborn, by Ahinoam of Jezreel;

Daniel was born second, by Abigail of Carmel;

[2] Absalom son of Maacah, daughter of King Talmai of Geshur, was third;

Adonijah son of Haggith was fourth;

[3] Shephatiah, by Abital, was fifth;

and Ithream, by David's wife Eglah, was sixth.

[4] Six sons were born to David in Hebron, where he reigned seven years and six months, and he reigned in Jerusalem thirty-three years.

[5] These sons were born to him in Jerusalem:

Shimea, Shobab, Nathan, and Solomon. These four were born to him by Bath-shua daughter of Ammiel.

[6] David's other sons: Ibhar, Elishua, Eliphelet, [7] Nogah, Nepheg, Japhia, [8] Elishama, Eliada, and Eliphelet—nine sons.

[9] These were all David's sons, with their sister Tamar, in addition to the sons by his concubines.

Judah's Kings

[10] Solomon's son was Rehoboam;

his son was Abijah, his son Asa,

his son Jehoshaphat, [11] his son Jehoram,

his son Ahaziah, his son Joash,

[12] his son Amaziah, his son Azariah,

his son Jotham, [13] his son Ahaz,

his son Hezekiah, his son Manasseh,

[14] his son Amon, and his son Josiah.

[15] Josiah's sons:

Johanan was the firstborn, Jehoiakim second,

Zedekiah third, and Shallum fourth.

[16] Jehoiakim's sons:

his sons Jeconiah and Zedekiah.

David's Line After the Exile

[17] The sons of Jeconiah the captive:

his sons Shealtiel, [18] Malchiram, Pedaiah, Shenazzar, Jekamiah, Hoshama, and Nedabiah.

[19] Pedaiah's sons: Zerubbabel and Shimei.

Zerubbabel's sons: Meshullam and Hananiah, with their sister Shelomith; [20] and five others—Hashubah, Ohel, Berechiah, Hasadiah, and Jushab-hesed.

[21] Hananiah's descendants: Pelatiah, Jeshaiah, and the sons of Rephaiah, Arnan, Obadiah, and Shecaniah.

[22] The son of Shecaniah: Shemaiah.

Shemaiah's sons: Hattush, Igal, Bariah, Neariah, and Shaphat—six.

[23] Neariah's sons: Elioenai, Hizkiah, and Azrikam—three.

[24] Elioenai's sons: Hodaviah, Eliashib, Pelaiah, Akkub, Johanan, Delaiah, and Anani—seven.

1 CHRONICLES 4

Judah's Descendants

[1] Judah's sons: Perez, Hezron, Carmi, Hur, and Shobal.

[2] Reaiah son of Shobal fathered Jahath, and Jahath fathered Ahumai and Lahad.

These were the families of the Zorathites.

[3] These were Etam's sons: Jezreel, Ishma, and Idbash, and their sister was named Hazzelelponi.

[4] Penuel fathered Gedor, and Ezer fathered Hushah.

These were the sons of Hur, Ephrathah's firstborn and the father of Bethlehem:

[5] Ashhur fathered Tekoa and had two wives, Helah and Naarah.

[6] Naarah bore Ahuzzam, Hepher, Temeni, and Haahashtari to him. These were Naarah's sons.

[7] Helah's sons: Zereth, Zohar, and Ethnan. [8] Koz fathered Anub, Zobebah, and the families of Aharhel son of Harum.

[9] Jabez was more honored than his brothers. His mother named him Jabez and said, "I gave birth to him in pain."

[10] Jabez called out to the God of Israel, "If only you would bless me, extend my border, let your hand be with me, and keep me from harm, so that I will not experience pain." And God granted his request.

[11] Chelub brother of Shuhah fathered Mehir, who was the father of Eshton. [12] Eshton fathered Beth-rapha, Paseah, and Tehinnah the father of Irnahash. These were the men of Recah. [13] Kenaz's sons: Othniel and Seraiah.

Othniel's sons: Hathath and Meonothai. [14] Meonothai fathered Ophrah,

and Seraiah fathered Joab, the ancestor of those in the Craftsmen's Valley, for they were craftsmen. [15] The sons of Caleb son of Jephunneh: Iru, Elah, and Naam.

Elah's son: Kenaz. [16] Jehallelel's sons: Ziph, Ziphah, Tiria, and Asarel. [17] Ezrah's sons: Jether, Mered, Epher, and Jalon. Mered's wife Bithiah gave birth to Miriam, Shammai, and Ishbah the father of Eshtemoa. [18] These were the sons of Pharaoh's daughter Bithiah; Mered had married her. His Judean wife gave birth to Jered the father of Gedor, Heber the father of Soco, and Jekuthiel the father of Zanoah. [19] The sons of Hodiah's wife, the sister of Naham: the father of Keilah the Garmite and the father of Eshtemoa the Maacathite. [20] Shimon's sons: Amnon, Rinnah, Ben-hanan, and Tilon.

Ishi's sons: Zoheth and Ben-zoheth.

[21] The sons of Shelah son of Judah: Er the father of Lecah, Laadah the father of Mareshah, the families of the guild of linen workers at Beth-ashbea, [22] Jokim, the men of Cozeba; and Joash and Saraph, who married Moabites and returned to Lehem. These names are from ancient records. [23] They were the potters and residents of Netaim and Gederah. They lived there in the service of the king.

Simeon's Descendants

[24] Simeon's sons: Nemuel, Jamin, Jarib, Zerah, and Shaul; [25] Shaul's sons: his son Shallum, his son Mibsam, and his son Mishma. [26] Mishma's sons: his son Hammuel, his son Zaccur, and his son Shimei.

[27] Shimei had sixteen sons and six daughters, but his brothers did not have many children, so their whole family did not become as numerous as the Judeans. [28] They lived in Beer-sheba, Moladah, Hazar-shual, [29] Bilhah, Ezem, Tolad, [30] Bethuel, Hormah, Ziklag, [31] Beth-marcaboth, Hazar-susim, Beth-biri, and Shaaraim. These were their cities until David became king. [32] Their villages were Etam, Ain, Rimmon, Tochen, and Ashan—five cities, [33] and all their surrounding villages as far as Baal. These were their settlements, and they kept a genealogical record for themselves.

[34] Meshobab, Jamlech, Joshah son of Amaziah, [35] Joel, Jehu son of Joshibiah, son of Seraiah, son of Asiel, [36] Elioenai, Jaakobah, Jeshohaiah, Asaiah, Adiel, Jesimiel, Benaiah, [37] and Ziza son of Shiphi, son of Allon, son of Jedaiah, son of Shimri, son of Shemaiah—

³⁸ these mentioned by name were leaders in their families. Their ancestral houses increased greatly. ³⁹ They went to the entrance of Gedor, to the east side of the valley to seek pasture for their flocks. ⁴⁰ They found rich, good pasture, and the land was broad, peaceful, and quiet, for some Hamites had lived there previously.

⁴¹ These who were recorded by name came in the days of King Hezekiah of Judah, attacked the Hamites' tents and the Meunites who were found there, and set them apart for destruction, as they are today. Then they settled in their place because there was pasture for their flocks. ⁴² Now five hundred men from these sons of Simeon went with Pelatiah, Neariah, Rephaiah, and Uzziel, the descendants of Ishi, as their leaders to Mount Seir. ⁴³ They struck down the remnant of the Amalekites who had escaped, and they still live there today.

🔖 GOING DEEPER

MARK 11:9–10

⁹ Those who went ahead and those who followed shouted:

> *Hosanna!*
> Blessed is he who comes
> in the name of the Lord!
> ¹⁰ Blessed is the coming kingdom
> of our father David!
> *Hosanna* in the highest heaven!

The Genealogy of the Levites

1 CHRONICLES 5

Reuben's Descendants

[1] These were the sons of Reuben the firstborn of Israel. He was the firstborn, but his birthright was given to the sons of Joseph son of Israel, because Reuben defiled his father's bed. He is not listed in the genealogy according to birthright. [2] Although Judah became strong among his brothers and a ruler came from him, the birthright was given to Joseph.

[3] The sons of Reuben, Israel's firstborn:

Hanoch, Pallu, Hezron, and Carmi.

[4] Joel's sons: his son Shemaiah,

his son Gog, his son Shimei,

[5] his son Micah, his son Reaiah,

his son Baal, [6] and his son Beerah.

Beerah was a leader of the Reubenites, and King Tiglath-pileser of Assyria took him into exile. [7] His relatives by their families as they are recorded in their family records:

Jeiel the chief, Zechariah,

[8] and Bela son of Azaz,

son of Shema, son of Joel.

They settled in Aroer as far as Nebo and Baal-meon. [9] They also settled in the east as far as the edge of the desert that extends to the Euphrates River, because their herds had increased in the land of Gilead. [10] During Saul's reign they waged war against the Hagrites, who were defeated by their power. And they lived in their tents throughout the region east of Gilead.

Gad's Descendants

[11] The sons of Gad lived next to them in the land of Bashan as far as Salecah:

[12] Joel the chief, Shapham the second in command, Janai, and Shaphat in Bashan.

[13] Their relatives according to their ancestral houses: Michael, Meshullam, Sheba, Jorai, Jacan, Zia, and Eber—seven.

[14] These were the sons of Abihail son of Huri,

son of Jaroah, son of Gilead,

son of Michael, son of Jeshishai,

son of Jahdo, son of Buz.

[15] Ahi son of Abdiel, son of Guni, was head of their ancestral family. [16] They lived in Gilead, in Bashan and its surrounding villages, and throughout the pasturelands of

Sharon. [17] All of them were registered in the genealogies during the reigns of Judah's King Jotham and Israel's King Jeroboam.

[18] The descendants of Reuben and Gad and half the tribe of Manasseh had 44,760 warriors who could serve in the army—men who carried shield and sword, drew the bow, and were trained for war. [19] They waged war against the Hagrites, Jetur, Naphish, and Nodab. [20] They received help against these enemies because they cried out to God in battle, and the Hagrites and all their allies were handed over to them. He was receptive to their prayer because they trusted in him. [21] They captured the Hagrites' livestock—fifty thousand of their camels, two hundred fifty thousand sheep, and two thousand donkeys—as well as one hundred thousand people. [22] Many of the Hagrites were killed because it was God's battle. And they lived there in the Hagrites' place until the exile.

Half the Tribe of Manasseh

[23] The descendants of half the tribe of Manasseh settled in the land from Bashan to Baal-hermon (that is, Senir or Mount Hermon); they were numerous. [24] These were the heads of their ancestral families: Epher, Ishi, Eliel, Azriel, Jeremiah, Hodaviah, and Jahdiel. They were valiant warriors, famous men, and heads of their ancestral houses. [25] But they were unfaithful to the God of their ancestors. They prostituted themselves with the gods of the nations God had destroyed before them. [26] So the God of Israel roused the spirit of King Pul (that is, Tiglath-pileser) of Assyria, and he took the Reubenites, Gadites, and half the tribe of Manasseh into exile. He took them to Halah, Habor, Hara, and Gozan's river, where they are until today.

1 CHRONICLES 6

The Levites → great-grandfather of MOSES (who led I out of Egypt)
— sold brother in slavery to egypt

[1] Levi's sons: Gershom, Kohath, and Merari.

[2] Kohath's sons: Amram, Izhar, Hebron, and Uzziel.

[3] Amram's children: Aaron, Moses, and Miriam.

Aaron's sons: Nadab, Abihu, Eleazar, and Ithamar.

[4] Eleazar fathered Phinehas;

Phinehas fathered Abishua;

[5] Abishua fathered Bukki;

Bukki fathered Uzzi;

⁶ Uzzi fathered Zerahiah;

Zerahiah fathered Meraioth;

⁷ Meraioth fathered Amariah;

Amariah fathered Ahitub;

⁸ Ahitub fathered Zadok;

Zadok fathered Ahimaaz;

⁹ Ahimaaz fathered Azariah;

Azariah fathered Johanan;

¹⁰ Johanan fathered Azariah, who served as priest in the temple that Solomon built in Jerusalem;

¹¹ Azariah fathered Amariah;

Amariah fathered Ahitub;

¹² Ahitub fathered Zadok;

Zadok fathered Shallum;

¹³ Shallum fathered Hilkiah;

Hilkiah fathered Azariah;

¹⁴ Azariah fathered Seraiah;

and Seraiah fathered Jehozadak.

¹⁵ Jehozadak went into exile when the LORD sent Judah and Jerusalem into exile at the hands of Nebuchadnezzar.

¹⁶ Levi's sons: Gershom, Kohath, and Merari.

¹⁷ These are the names of Gershom's sons: Libni and Shimei.

¹⁸ Kohath's sons: Amram, Izhar, Hebron and Uzziel.

¹⁹ Merari's sons: Mahli and Mushi.

These are the Levites' families according to their fathers:

²⁰ Of Gershom: his son Libni,

his son Jahath, his son Zimmah,

²¹ his son Joah, his son Iddo,

his son Zerah, and his son Jeatherai.

²² Kohath's sons: his son Amminadab,

his son Korah, his son Assir,

²³ his son Elkanah, his son Ebiasaph,

his son Assir, ²⁴ his son Tahath,

his son Uriel, his son Uzziah,

and his son Shaul.

²⁵ Elkanah's sons: Amasai and Ahimoth,

²⁶ his son Elkanah, his son Zophai,

his son Nahath, ²⁷ his son Eliab,

his son Jeroham, and his son Elkanah.

²⁸ Samuel's sons: his firstborn Joel,

and his second son Abijah.

²⁹ Merari's sons: Mahli, his son Libni,

his son Shimei, his son Uzzah,

³⁰ his son Shimea, his son Haggiah,

and his son Asaiah.

The Musicians

³¹ These are the men David put in charge of the music in the LORD's temple after the ark came to rest there. ³² They ministered with song in front of the tabernacle, the tent of meeting, until Solomon built the LORD's temple in Jerusalem, and they performed their task according to the regulations given to them. ³³ These are the men who served with their sons.

From the Kohathites: Heman the singer,

son of Joel, son of Samuel,

³⁴ son of Elkanah, son of Jeroham,

son of Eliel, son of Toah,

³⁵ son of Zuph, son of Elkanah,

son of Mahath, son of Amasai,

³⁶ son of Elkanah, son of Joel,

son of Azariah, son of Zephaniah,

³⁷ son of Tahath, son of Assir,

son of Ebiasaph, son of Korah,

³⁸ son of Izhar, son of Kohath,

son of Levi, son of Israel.

³⁹ Heman's relative was Asaph, who stood at his right hand:

Asaph son of Berechiah, son of Shimea,

⁴⁰ son of Michael, son of Baaseiah,

son of Malchijah, ⁴¹ son of Ethni,

son of Zerah, son of Adaiah,

⁴² son of Ethan, son of Zimmah,

son of Shimei, ⁴³ son of Jahath,

son of Gershom, son of Levi.

⁴⁴ On the left, their relatives were Merari's sons:

Ethan son of Kishi, son of Abdi,

son of Malluch, ⁴⁵ son of Hashabiah,

son of Amaziah, son of Hilkiah,

⁴⁶ son of Amzi, son of Bani,

son of Shemer, ⁴⁷ son of Mahli,

son of Mushi, son of Merari,

son of Levi.

Aaron's Descendants

⁴⁸ Their relatives, the Levites, were assigned to all the service of the tabernacle, God's temple. ⁴⁹ But Aaron and his sons did all the work of the most holy place. They presented the offerings on the altar of burnt offerings and on the altar of incense to make atonement for Israel according to all that Moses the servant of God had commanded.

⁵⁰ These are Aaron's sons: his son Eleazar, his son Phinehas, his son Abishua, ⁵¹ his son Bukki, his son Uzzi, his son Zerahiah, ⁵² his son Meraioth, his son Amariah, his son Ahitub, ⁵³ his son Zadok, and his son Ahimaaz.

The Settlements of the Levites

⁵⁴ These were the places assigned to Aaron's descendants from the Kohathite family for their settlements in their territory, because the first lot was for them. ⁵⁵ They were given Hebron in the land of Judah and its surrounding pasturelands, ⁵⁶ but the fields and settlements around the city were given to Caleb son of Jephunneh. ⁵⁷ Aaron's descendants were given:

Hebron (a city of refuge), Libnah and its pasturelands, Jattir, Eshtemoa and its pasturelands, ⁵⁸ Hilen and its pasturelands, Debir and its pasturelands, ⁵⁹ Ashan and its pasturelands, and Beth-shemesh and its pasturelands. ⁶⁰ From the tribe of Benjamin they were given Geba and its pasturelands, Alemeth and its pasturelands, and Anathoth and its pasturelands. They had thirteen towns in all among their families.

⁶¹ To the rest of the Kohathites, ten towns from half the tribe of Manasseh were assigned by lot.

⁶² The Gershomites were assigned thirteen towns from the tribes of Issachar, Asher, Naphtali, and Manasseh in Bashan according to their families.

⁶³ The Merarites were assigned by lot twelve towns from the tribes of Reuben, Gad, and Zebulun according to their families. ⁶⁴ So the Israelites gave these towns and their pasturelands to the Levites. ⁶⁵ They assigned by lot the towns named above from the tribes of the descendants of Judah, Simeon, and Benjamin.

⁶⁶ Some of the families of the Kohathites were given towns from the tribe of Ephraim for their territory:

⁶⁷ Shechem (a city of refuge) with its pasturelands in the hill country of Ephraim, Gezer and its pasturelands, ⁶⁸ Jokmeam and its pasturelands, Beth-horon and its pasturelands, ⁶⁹ Aijalon and its pasturelands, and Gath-rimmon and its pasturelands. ⁷⁰ From half the tribe of Manasseh, Aner and its pasturelands, and Bileam and its pasturelands were given to the rest of the families of the Kohathites.

⁷¹ The Gershomites received:

Golan in Bashan and its pasturelands, and Ashtaroth and its pasturelands from the families of half the tribe of Manasseh. ⁷² From the tribe of Issachar they received Kedesh and its pasturelands, Daberath and its pasturelands, ⁷³ Ramoth and its pasturelands, and Anem and its pasturelands. ⁷⁴ From the tribe of Asher they received Mashal and its pasturelands, Abdon and its pasturelands, ⁷⁵ Hukok and its pasturelands, and Rehob and its pasturelands. ⁷⁶ From the tribe of Naphtali they received Kedesh in Galilee and its pasturelands, Hammon and its pasturelands, and Kiriathaim and its pasturelands.

⁷⁷ The rest of the Merarites received:

From the tribe of Zebulun they received Rimmono and its pasturelands and Tabor and its pasturelands. ⁷⁸ From the tribe of Reuben across the Jordan at Jericho, to the east of the Jordan, they received Bezer in the desert and its pasturelands, Jahzah and its pasturelands, ⁷⁹ Kedemoth and its pasturelands, and Mephaath and its pasturelands. ⁸⁰ From the tribe of Gad they received Ramoth in Gilead and its pasturelands, Mahanaim and its pasturelands, ⁸¹ Heshbon and its pasturelands, and Jazer and its pasturelands.

◆ GOING DEEPER

DEUTERONOMY 10:8-9

⁸ At that time the LORD set apart the tribe of Levi to carry the ark of the LORD's covenant, to stand before the LORD to serve him, and to pronounce blessings in his name, as it is today. ⁹ For this reason, Levi does not have a portion or inheritance like his brothers; the LORD is his inheritance, as the LORD your God told him

The Genealogies of the Northern and Central Tribes

1 CHRONICLES 7

Issachar's Descendants

¹ Issachar's sons: Tola, Puah, Jashub, and Shimron—four.

² Tola's sons: Uzzi, Rephaiah, Jeriel, Jahmai, Ibsam, and Shemuel, the heads of their ancestral families. During David's reign, 22,600 descendants of Tola were recorded as valiant warriors in their family records.

³ Uzzi's son: Izrahiah.

Izrahiah's sons: Michael, Obadiah, Joel, Isshiah. All five of them were chiefs. ⁴ Along with them, they had 36,000 troops for battle according to the family records of their ancestral families, for they had many wives and children. ⁵ Their tribesmen who were valiant warriors belonging to all the families of Issachar totaled 87,000 in their genealogies.

Benjamin's Descendants

⁶ Three of Benjamin's sons: Bela, Becher, and Jediael.

⁷ Bela's sons: Ezbon, Uzzi, Uzziel, Jerimoth, and Iri—five.

They were valiant warriors and heads of their ancestral families; 22,034 were listed in their genealogies. [8] Becher's sons: Zemirah, Joash, Eliezer, Elioenai, Omri, Jeremoth, Abijah, Anathoth, and Alemeth; all these were Becher's sons. [9] Their family records were recorded according to the heads of their ancestral families—20,200 valiant warriors. [10] Jediael's son: Bilhan.

Bilhan's sons: Jeush, Benjamin, Ehud, Chenaanah, Zethan, Tarshish, and Ahishahar. [11] All these sons of Jediael listed by family heads were valiant warriors; there were 17,200 who could serve in the army. [12] Shuppim and Huppim were sons of Ir, and the Hushim were the sons of Aher.

Naphtali's Descendants

[13] Naphtali's sons: Jahziel, Guni, Jezer, and Shallum—Bilhah's sons.

Manasseh's Descendants

[14] Manasseh's sons through his Aramean concubine: Asriel and Machir the father of Gilead. [15] Machir took wives from Huppim and Shuppim. The name of his sister was Maacah. Another descendant was named Zelophehad, but he had only daughters.

[16] Machir's wife Maacah gave birth to a son, and she named him Peresh. His brother was named Sheresh, and his sons were Ulam and Rekem.

[17] Ulam's son: Bedan. These were the sons of Gilead son of Machir, son of Manasseh. [18] His sister Hammolecheth gave birth to Ishhod, Abiezer, and Mahlah.

[19] Shemida's sons: Ahian, Shechem, Likhi, and Aniam.

Ephraim's Descendants

[20] Ephraim's sons: Shuthelah, and his son Bered, his son Tahath, his son Eleadah,

his son Tahath, [21] his son Zabad,

his son Shuthelah, also Ezer, and Elead.

The men of Gath, born in the land, killed them because they went down to raid their cattle. [22] Their father Ephraim mourned a long time, and his relatives came to comfort him. [23] He slept with his wife, and she conceived and gave birth to a son. So he named him Beriah, because there had been misfortune in his home. [24] His daughter was Sheerah, who built Lower and Upper Beth-horon and Uzzen-sheerah,

[25] his son Rephah, his son Resheph,

his son Telah, his son Tahan,

[26] his son Ladan, his son Ammihud,

his son Elishama, [27] his son Nun,

and his son Joshua.

[28] Their holdings and settlements were Bethel and its surrounding villages; Naaran to the east, Gezer and its villages to the west, and Shechem and its villages as far as Ayyah and its villages, [29] and along the borders of the descendants of Manasseh, Beth-shean, Taanach, Megiddo, and Dor with their surrounding villages. The sons of Joseph son of Israel lived in these towns.

Asher's Descendants

[30] Asher's sons: Imnah, Ishvah, Ishvi, and Beriah, with their sister Serah.

[31] Beriah's sons: Heber, and Malchiel, who fathered Birzaith.

[32] Heber fathered Japhlet, Shomer, and Hotham, with their sister Shua.

[33] Japhlet's sons: Pasach, Bimhal, and Ashvath. These were Japhlet's sons.

[34] Shemer's sons: Ahi, Rohgah, Hubbah, and Aram.

[35] His brother Helem's sons: Zophah, Imna, Shelesh, and Amal.

[36] Zophah's sons: Suah, Harnepher, Shual, Beri, Imrah, [37] Bezer, Hod, Shamma, Shilshah, Ithran, and Beera.

[38] Jether's sons: Jephunneh, Pispa, and Ara.

[39] Ulla's sons: Arah, Hanniel, and Rizia.

[40] All these were Asher's descendants. They were the heads of their ancestral families, chosen men, valiant warriors, and chiefs among the leaders. The number of men listed in their genealogies for military service was 26,000.

Benjamin's Descendants

[1] Benjamin fathered Bela, his firstborn; Ashbel was born second, Aharah third, [2] Nohah fourth, and Rapha fifth.

[3] Bela's sons: Addar, Gera, Abihud, [4] Abishua, Naaman, Ahoah, [5] Gera, Shephuphan, and Huram.

[6] These were Ehud's sons, who were the heads of the families living in Geba and who were deported to Manahath: [7] Naaman, Ahijah, and Gera. Gera deported them and was the father of Uzza and Ahihud.

[8] Shaharaim had sons in the territory of Moab after he had divorced his wives Hushim and Baara. [9] His sons by his wife Hodesh: Jobab, Zibia, Mesha, Malcam, [10] Jeuz, Sachia, and Mirmah. These were his sons, family heads. [11] He also had sons by Hushim: Abitub and Elpaal.

[12] Elpaal's sons: Eber, Misham, and Shemed who built Ono and Lod and its surrounding villages, [13] Beriah and Shema, who were the family heads of Aijalon's residents and who drove out the residents of Gath, [14] Ahio, Shashak, and Jeremoth.

[15] Zebadiah, Arad, Eder, [16] Michael, Ishpah, and Joha were Beriah's sons.

[17] Zebadiah, Meshullam, Hizki, Heber, [18] Ishmerai, Izliah, and Jobab were Elpaal's sons.

[19] Jakim, Zichri, Zabdi, [20] Elienai, Zillethai, Eliel, [21] Adaiah, Beraiah, and Shimrath were Shimei's sons.

[22] Ishpan, Eber, Eliel, [23] Abdon, Zichri, Hanan, [24] Hananiah, Elam, Anthothijah, [25] Iphdeiah, and Penuel were Shashak's sons.

[26] Shamsherai, Shehariah, Athaliah, [27] Jaareshiah, Elijah, and Zichri were Jeroham's sons.

[28] These were family heads, chiefs according to their family records; they lived in Jerusalem.

[29] Jeiel fathered Gibeon and lived in Gibeon. His wife's name was Maacah. [30] Abdon was his firstborn son, then Zur, Kish, Baal, Nadab, [31] Gedor, Ahio, Zecher, [32] and Mikloth who fathered Shimeah. These also lived opposite their relatives in Jerusalem, with their other relatives.

[33] Ner fathered Kish, Kish fathered Saul, and Saul fathered Jonathan, Malchishua, Abinadab, and Esh-baal.

[34] Jonathan's son was Merib-baal, and Merib-baal fathered Micah.

[35] Micah's sons: Pithon, Melech, Tarea, and Ahaz.

36 Ahaz fathered Jehoaddah, Jehoaddah fathered Alemeth, Azmaveth, and Zimri, and Zimri fathered Moza.

37 Moza fathered Binea. His son was Raphah, his son Elasah, and his son Azel.

38 Azel had six sons, and these were their names: Azrikam, Bocheru, Ishmael, Sheariah, Obadiah, and Hanan. All these were Azel's sons.

39 His brother Eshek's sons: Ulam was his firstborn, Jeush second, and Eliphelet third.

40 Ulam's sons were valiant warriors and archers. They had many sons and grandsons—150 of them.

All these were among Benjamin's sons.

🔖 GOING DEEPER

DEUTERONOMY 33:12

He said about Benjamin:

The LORD's beloved rests securely on him.
He shields him all day long,
and he rests on his shoulders.

WEEK 1   DAY 5

Resettlement in Jerusalem

1 CHRONICLES 9

After the Exile

¹ All Israel was registered in the genealogies that are written in the Book of the Kings of Israel. But Judah was exiled to Babylon because of their unfaithfulness. ² The first to live in their towns on their own property again were Israelites, priests, Levites, and temple servants.

³ These people from the descendants of Judah, Benjamin, Ephraim, and Manasseh settled in Jerusalem:

⁴ Uthai son of Ammihud, son of Omri, son of Imri, son of Bani, a descendant of Perez son of Judah;

⁵ from the Shilonites:

Asaiah the firstborn and his sons;

⁶ and from the descendants of Zerah:

Jeuel and their relatives—690 in all.

⁷ The Benjaminites: Sallu son of Meshullam, son of Hodaviah, son of Hassenuah;

⁸ Ibneiah son of Jeroham;

Elah son of Uzzi, son of Michri;

Meshullam son of Shephatiah, son of Reuel, son of Ibnijah;

⁹ and their relatives according to their family records—956 in all. All these men were heads of their ancestral families.

¹⁰ The priests: Jedaiah; Jehoiarib; Jachin;

¹¹ Azariah son of Hilkiah, son of Meshullam, son of Zadok, son of Meraioth, son of Ahitub, the chief official of God's temple;

¹² Adaiah son of Jeroham, son of Pashhur, son of Malchijah; Maasai son of Adiel, son of Jahzerah, son of Meshullam, son of Meshillemith, son of Immer;

¹³ and their relatives, the heads of their ancestral families—1,760 in all. They were capable men employed in the ministry of God's temple.

¹⁴ The Levites: Shemaiah son of Hasshub, son of Azrikam, son of Hashabiah of the Merarites;

¹⁵ Bakbakkar, Heresh, Galal, and Mattaniah, son of Mica, son of Zichri, son of Asaph;

¹⁶ Obadiah son of Shemaiah, son of Galal, son of Jeduthun; and Berechiah son of Asa, son of Elkanah who lived in the settlements of the Netophathites.

¹⁷ The gatekeepers: Shallum, Akkub, Talmon, Ahiman, and their relatives.

Shallum was their chief; [18] he was previously stationed at the King's Gate on the east side. These were the gatekeepers from the camp of the Levites.

[19] Shallum son of Kore, son of Ebiasaph, son of Korah and his relatives from his ancestral family, the Korahites, were assigned to guard the thresholds of the tent. Their ancestors had been assigned to the LORD's camp as guardians of the entrance. [20] In earlier times Phinehas son of Eleazar had been their leader, and the LORD was with him. [21] Zechariah son of Meshelemiah was the gatekeeper at the entrance to the tent of meeting.

[22] The total number of those chosen to be gatekeepers at the thresholds was 212. They were registered by genealogy in their settlements. David and the seer Samuel had appointed them to their trusted positions. [23] So they and their sons were assigned as guards to the gates of the LORD's temple, which had been the tent-temple. [24] The gatekeepers were on the four sides: east, west, north, and south. [25] Their relatives came from their settlements at fixed times to be with them seven days, [26] but the four chief gatekeepers, who were Levites, were entrusted with the rooms and the treasuries of God's temple. [27] They spent the night in the vicinity of God's temple, because they had guard duty and were in charge of opening it every morning.

[28] Some of them were in charge of the utensils used in worship. They would count them when they brought them in and when they took them out. [29] Others were put in charge of the furnishings and all the utensils of the sanctuary, as well as the fine flour, wine, oil, incense, and spices. [30] Some of the priests' sons mixed the spices. [31] A Levite called Mattithiah, the firstborn of Shallum the Korahite, was entrusted with baking the bread. [32] Some of the Kohathites' relatives were responsible for preparing the rows of the Bread of the Presence every Sabbath.

[33] The singers, the heads of the Levite families, stayed in the temple chambers and were exempt from other tasks because they were on duty day and night. [34] These were the heads of the Levite families, chiefs according to their family records; they lived in Jerusalem.

Saul's Family

[35] Jeiel fathered Gibeon and lived in Gibeon. His wife's name was Maacah. [36] Abdon was his firstborn son, then Zur, Kish, Baal, Ner, Nadab, [37] Gedor, Ahio, Zechariah, and Mikloth. [38] Mikloth fathered Shimeam. These also lived opposite their relatives in Jerusalem with their other relatives.

[39] Ner fathered Kish, Kish fathered Saul, and Saul fathered Jonathan, Malchishua, Abinadab, and Esh-baal.

[40] Jonathan's son was Merib-baal, and Merib-baal fathered Micah.

[41] Micah's sons: Pithon, Melech, Tahrea, and Ahaz.

[42] Ahaz fathered Jarah;

Jarah fathered Alemeth, Azmaveth, and Zimri;

Zimri fathered Moza.

[43] Moza fathered Binea.

His son was Rephaiah, his son Elasah, and his son Azel.

[44] Azel had six sons, and these were their names: Azrikam, Bocheru, Ishmael, Sheariah, Obadiah, and Hanan. These were Azel's sons.

GOING DEEPER

GALATIANS 3:28-29

[28] There is no Jew or Greek, slave or free, male and female; since you are all one in Christ Jesus.

[29] And if you belong to Christ, then you are Abraham's seed, heirs according to the promise.

Roasted Figs and Brussels Sprouts

Prep Time
15 MINUTES

Cook Time
35 MINUTES

Serves
2–3

INGREDIENTS

2 cups Brussels sprouts, trimmed and halved

1 small sweet onion, sliced

8 figs, halved

1½ tablespoons olive oil

Leaves from 6 sprigs of thyme

Salt and pepper, to taste

1 tablespoon aged balsamic vinegar

— Preheat oven to 400° F.

— Toss Brussels sprouts, onion, and figs with olive oil and place on a baking sheet lined with parchment paper. Sprinkle with thyme leaves, salt, and pepper.

— Roast for about 30 to 35 minutes, turning Brussels sprouts at least once to evenly roast.

— Once Brussels sprouts and onions caramelize and figs appear slightly shriveled, remove from the oven and coat with balsamic vinegar. Let cool for 5 minutes before serving.

DAY 6

WEEK 1

Grace Day

Your faithfulness is for all generations; you established the earth, and it stands firm.

PSALM 119:90

Take this day to catch up on your reading, pray, and rest in the presence of the Lord.

Weekly Truth

Scripture is God-breathed and true. When we memorize it, we carry His Word with us wherever we go.

During this plan, we will work to memorize 1 Chronicles 29:11–13, part of David's prayer of blessing. This week we will memorize the first part of verse 11, where David acknowledges that everything belongs to God.

See tips for memorizing Scripture on page 240.

Yours, LORD, is the greatness and the power and the glory and the splendor and the majesty, for everything in the heavens and on earth belongs to you. Yours, LORD, is the kingdom, and you are exalted as head over all. Riches and honor come from you, and you are the ruler of everything. Power and might are in your hand, and it is in your hand to make great and to give strength to all. Now therefore, our God, we give you thanks and praise your glorious name.

1 CHRONICLES 29:11-13

HIS FAITHFUL PROMISES ARE Your Armor & PROTECTION

Those who live in the Shelter of the most HIGH will FIND REST in the Shadow of the ALMIGHTY

He will Cover you WITH HIS FEATHERS.

He will Shelter you WITH HIS WINGS.

God's People United

1 CHRONICLES 10–29; 2 CHRONICLES 1–9

Surrender

Jesus, I know that following you does not protect me from difficulty or disaster

bUt I thank you that I am never ALONE ... even when the worst happens.

Today ... I choose to place my TRUST in you whatever my future may hold.

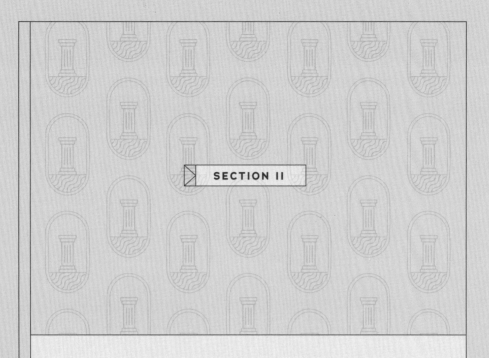

SECTION II

Following the genealogies, the Chronicler moves to retelling the portion of Israel's history as a united kingdom under the reigns of Saul, David, and Solomon. God's people were identified by two realities: covenant relationship with God and the proper worship that was an overflow of this relationship. David's desire to build the temple and Solomon's completion of the temple represented the importance of worship as a central practice and identifier for the people of God.

GOD'S
PEOPLE
UNITED

David's Anointing as King

DAY 8

WEEK 2

1 CHRONICLES 10

The Death of Saul and His Sons

[1] The Philistines fought against Israel, and Israel's men fled from them. Many were killed on Mount Gilboa. [2] The Philistines pursued Saul and his sons and killed his sons Jonathan, Abinadab, and Malchishua. [3] When the battle intensified against Saul, the archers spotted him and severely wounded him. [4] Then Saul said to his armor-bearer, "Draw your sword and run me through with it, or these uncircumcised men will come and torture me." But his armor-bearer would not do it because he was terrified. Then Saul took his sword and fell on it. [5] When his armor-bearer saw that Saul was dead, he also fell on his own sword and died. [6] So Saul and his three sons died—his whole house died together.

[7] When all the men of Israel in the valley saw that the army had fled and that Saul and his sons were dead, they abandoned their cities and fled. So the Philistines came and settled in them.

[8] The next day when the Philistines came to strip the slain, they found Saul and his sons dead on Mount Gilboa. [9] They stripped Saul, cut off his head, took his armor, and sent messengers throughout the land of the Philistines to spread the good news to their idols and the people. [10] Then they put his armor in the temple of their gods and hung his skull in the temple of Dagon.

[11] When all Jabesh-gilead heard of everything the Philistines had done to Saul, [12] all their brave men set out and retrieved the body of Saul and the bodies of his sons and brought them to Jabesh. They buried their bones under the oak in Jabesh and fasted seven days.

[13] Saul died for his unfaithfulness to the LORD because he did not keep the LORD's word. He even consulted a medium for guidance, [14] but he did not inquire of the LORD. So the LORD put him to death and turned the kingdom over to David son of Jesse.

1 CHRONICLES 11

David's Anointing as King

[1] All Israel came together to David at Hebron and said, "Here we are, your own flesh and blood. [2] Even previously when Saul was king, you were leading Israel out to battle and bringing us back. The LORD your God also said to you, 'You will shepherd my people Israel, and you will be ruler over my people Israel.'"

[3] So all the elders of Israel came to the king at Hebron. David made a covenant with them at Hebron in the LORD's presence, and they anointed David king over Israel, in keeping with the LORD's word through Samuel.

David's Capture of Jerusalem

[4] David and all Israel marched to Jerusalem (that is, Jebus); the Jebusites who inhabited the land were there. [5] The inhabitants of Jebus said to David, "You will never get in here." Yet David did capture the stronghold of Zion, that is, the city of David.

[6] David said, "Whoever is the first to kill a Jebusite will become chief commander." Joab son of Zeruiah went up first, so he became the chief.

[7] Then David took up residence in the stronghold; therefore, it was called the city of David.

[8] He built up the city all the way around, from the supporting terraces to the surrounding parts, and Joab restored the rest of the city. [9] David steadily grew more powerful, and the LORD of Armies was with him.

Exploits of David's Warriors

[10] The following were the chiefs of David's warriors who, together with all Israel, strongly supported him in his reign to make him king according to the LORD's word about Israel. [11] This is the list of David's warriors:

Jashobeam son of Hachmoni was chief of the Thirty; he wielded his spear against three hundred and killed them at one time.

[12] After him, Eleazar son of Dodo the Ahohite was one of the three warriors. [13] He was with David at Pas-dammim when the Philistines had gathered there for battle. There was a portion of a field full of barley, where the troops had fled from the Philistines. [14] But Eleazar and David took their stand in the middle of the field and defended it. They killed the Philistines, and the LORD gave them a great victory.

[15] Three of the thirty chief men went down to David, to the rock at the cave of Adullam, while the Philistine army was encamped in Rephaim Valley. [16] At that time David was in the stronghold, and a Philistine garrison was at Bethlehem. [17] David was extremely thirsty and said, "If only someone would bring me water to drink from the well at the city gate of Bethlehem!" [18] So the Three broke through the Philistine camp and drew water from the well at the gate of Bethlehem. They brought it back to David, but he refused to drink it. Instead, he poured it out to the LORD. [19] David said, "I would never do such a thing in the presence of my God! How can I drink the blood of these men who risked their lives?" For they brought it at the risk of their lives. So he would not drink it. Such were the exploits of the three warriors.

[20] Abishai, Joab's brother, was the leader of the Three. He raised his spear against three hundred men and killed them, gaining a reputation among the Three. [21] He was more honored than the Three and became their commander even though he did not become one of the Three.

[22] Benaiah son of Jehoiada was the son of a brave man from Kabzeel, a man of many exploits. Benaiah killed two sons of Ariel of Moab, and he went down into a pit on a snowy day and killed a lion. [23] He also killed an Egyptian who was seven and a half feet tall. Even though the Egyptian had a spear in his hand like a weaver's beam, Benaiah went down to him with a staff, snatched the spear out of the Egyptian's hand, and then killed him with his own spear. [24] These were the exploits of Benaiah son of Jehoiada, who had a reputation among the three warriors. [25] He was the most honored of the Thirty, but he did not become one of the Three. David put him in charge of his bodyguard.

[26] The best soldiers were
Joab's brother Asahel,
Elhanan son of Dodo of Bethlehem,
[27] Shammoth the Harorite,
Helez the Pelonite,
[28] Ira son of Ikkesh the Tekoite,
Abiezer the Anathothite,
[29] Sibbecai the Hushathite,
Ilai the Ahohite,
[30] Maharai the Netophathite,
Heled son of Baanah the Netophathite,
[31] Ithai son of Ribai from Gibeah of the Benjaminites,
Benaiah the Pirathonite,

32 Hurai from the wadis of Gaash,

Abiel the Arbathite,

33 Azmaveth the Baharumite,

Eliahba the Shaalbonite,

34 the sons of Hashem the Gizonite,

Jonathan son of Shagee the Hararite,

35 Ahiam son of Sachar the Hararite,

Eliphal son of Ur,

36 Hepher the Mecherathite,

Ahijah the Pelonite,

37 Hezro the Carmelite,

Naarai son of Ezbai,

38 Joel the brother of Nathan,

Mibhar son of Hagri,

39 Zelek the Ammonite,

Naharai the Beerothite, the armor-bearer for Joab
son of Zeruiah,

40 Ira the Ithrite,

Gareb the Ithrite,

41 Uriah the Hethite,

Zabad son of Ahlai,

42 Adina son of Shiza the Reubenite, chief of the Reubenites,
and thirty with him,

43 Hanan son of Maacah,

Joshaphat the Mithnite,

44 Uzzia the Ashterathite,

Shama and Jeiel the sons of Hotham the Aroerite,

45 Jediael son of Shimri and his brother Joha the Tizite,

46 Eliel the Mahavite,

Jeribai and Joshaviah, the sons of Elnaam,

Ithmah the Moabite,

47 Eliel, Obed, and Jaasiel the Mezobaite.

1 CHRONICLES 12

David's First Supporters

1 The following were the men who came to David at Ziklag while he was still banned from the presence of Saul son of Kish. They were among the warriors who helped him in battle. 2 They were archers who could use either the right or left hand, both to sling stones and shoot arrows from a bow. They were Saul's relatives from Benjamin:

3 Their chief was Ahiezer son of Shemaah the Gibeathite.

Then there was his brother Joash;

Jeziel and Pelet sons of Azmaveth;

Beracah, Jehu the Anathothite;

4 Ishmaiah the Gibeonite, a warrior among the Thirty and a
leader over the Thirty;

Jeremiah, Jahaziel, Johanan, Jozabad the Gederathite;

5 Eluzai, Jerimoth, Bealiah, Shemariah, Shephatiah
the Haruphite;

6 Elkanah, Isshiah, Azarel, Joezer, and Jashobeam,
the Korahites;

7 and Joelah and Zebadiah, the sons of Jeroham
from Gedor.

8 Some Gadites defected to David at his stronghold in the desert. They were valiant warriors, trained for battle, expert with shield and spear. Their faces were like the faces of lions, and they were as swift as gazelles on the mountains.

9 Ezer was the chief, Obadiah second, Eliab third,

10 Mishmannah fourth, Jeremiah fifth,

11 Attai sixth, Eliel seventh,

12 Johanan eighth, Elzabad ninth,

13 Jeremiah tenth, and Machbannai eleventh.

14 These Gadites were army commanders; the least of them was a match for a hundred, and the greatest of them for a thousand. 15 These are the men who crossed the Jordan in the first month when it was overflowing all its banks, and put to flight all those in the valleys to the east and to the west.

16 Other Benjaminites and men from Judah also went to David at the stronghold. 17 David went out to meet them and said to them, "If you have come in peace to help me, my heart will be united with you, but if you have come to betray me to my enemies even though my hands have done no wrong, may the God of our ancestors look on it and judge."

18 Then the Spirit enveloped Amasai, chief of the Thirty, and he said:

We are yours, David,
we are with you, son of Jesse!
Peace, peace to you,
and peace to him who helps you,
for your God helps you.

So David received them and made them leaders of his troops.

[19] Some Manassites defected to David when he went with the Philistines to fight against Saul. However, they did not help the Philistines because the Philistine rulers sent David away after a discussion. They said, "It will be our heads if he defects to his master Saul." [20] When David went to Ziklag, some men from Manasseh defected to him: Adnah, Jozabad, Jediael, Michael, Jozabad, Elihu, and Zillethai, chiefs of thousands in Manasseh. [21] They helped David against the raiders, for they were all valiant warriors and commanders in the army. [22] At that time, men came day after day to help David until there was a great army, like an army of God.

David's Soldiers in Hebron

[23] The numbers of the armed troops who came to David at Hebron to turn Saul's kingdom over to him, according to the LORD's word, were as follows:

[24] From the Judahites: 6,800 armed troops bearing shields and spears.

[25] From the Simeonites: 7,100 valiant warriors ready for war.

[26] From the Levites: 4,600 [27] in addition to Jehoiada, leader of the house of Aaron, with 3,700 men; [28] and Zadok, a young valiant warrior, with 22 commanders from his ancestral family.

[29] From the Benjaminites, the relatives of Saul: 3,000 (up to that time the majority of the Benjaminites maintained their allegiance to the house of Saul).

[30] From the Ephraimites: 20,800 valiant warriors who were famous men in their ancestral families.

[31] From half the tribe of Manasseh: 18,000 designated by name to come and make David king.

[32] From the Issacharites, who understood the times and knew what Israel should do: 200 chiefs with all their relatives under their command.

[33] From Zebulun: 50,000 who could serve in the army, trained for battle with all kinds of weapons of war, with one purpose to help David.

[34] From Naphtali: 1,000 commanders accompanied by 37,000 men with shield and spear.

[35] From the Danites: 28,600 trained for battle.

[36] From Asher: 40,000 who could serve in the army, trained for battle.

[37] From across the Jordan—from the Reubenites, Gadites, and half the tribe of Manasseh: 120,000 men equipped with all the military weapons of war.

[38] All these warriors, lined up in battle formation, came to Hebron wholeheartedly determined to make David king over all Israel. All the rest of Israel was also of one mind to make David king. [39] They spent three days there eating and drinking with David, for their relatives had provided for them. [40] In addition, their neighbors from as far away as Issachar, Zebulun, and Naphtali came and brought food on donkeys, camels, mules, and oxen—abundant provisions of flour, fig cakes, raisins, wine and oil, herds, and flocks. Indeed, there was joy in Israel.

GOING DEEPER

PSALM 78:70-72

[70] He chose David his servant
and took him from the sheep pens;
[71] he brought him from tending ewes
to be shepherd over his people Jacob—
over Israel, his inheritance.
[72] He shepherded them with a pure heart
and guided them with his skillful hands.

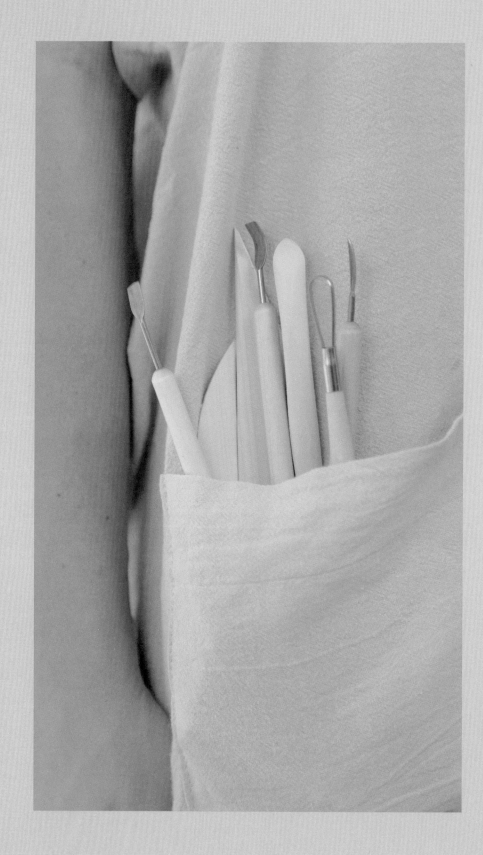

WEEK 2   DAY 9

David Moves the Ark of the Covenant

1 CHRONICLES 13

David and the Ark

¹ David consulted with all his leaders, the commanders of hundreds and of thousands. ² Then he said to the whole assembly of Israel, "If it seems good to you, and if this is from the LORD our God, let's spread out and send the message to the rest of our relatives in all the districts of Israel, including the priests and Levites in their cities with pasturelands, that they should gather together with us. ³ Then let's bring back the ark of our God, for we did not inquire of him in Saul's days." ⁴ Since the proposal seemed right to all the people, the whole assembly agreed to do it.

⁵ So David assembled all Israel, from the Shihor of Egypt to the entrance of Hamath, to bring the ark of God from Kiriath-jearim. ⁶ David and all Israel went to Baalah (that is, Kiriath-jearim that belongs to Judah) to take from there the ark of God, which bears the name of the LORD who is enthroned between the cherubim. ⁷ At Abinadab's house they set the ark of God on a new cart. Uzzah and Ahio were guiding the cart.

⁸ David and all Israel were dancing with all their might before God with songs and with lyres, harps, tambourines, cymbals, and trumpets. ⁹ When they came to Chidon's threshing floor, Uzzah reached out to hold the ark because the oxen had stumbled. ¹⁰ Then the LORD's anger burned against Uzzah, and he struck him dead because he had reached out to the ark. So he died there in the presence of God.

¹¹ David was angry because of the LORD's outburst against Uzzah, so he named that place Outburst Against Uzzah, as it is still named today. ¹² David feared God that day and said, "How can I ever bring the ark of God to me?" ¹³ So David did not bring the ark of God home to the city of David; instead, he diverted it to the house of Obed-edom of Gath. ¹⁴ The ark of God remained with Obed-edom's family in his house for three months, and the LORD blessed his family and all that he had.

1 CHRONICLES 14

God's Blessing on David

[1] King Hiram of Tyre sent envoys to David, along with cedar logs, stonemasons, and carpenters to build a palace for him. [2] Then David knew that the LORD had established him as king over Israel and that his kingdom had been exalted for the sake of his people Israel.

[3] David took more wives in Jerusalem, and he became the father of more sons and daughters. [4] These are the names of the children born to him in Jerusalem: Shammua, Shobab, Nathan, Solomon, [5] Ibhar, Elishua, Elpelet, [6] Nogah, Nepheg, Japhia, [7] Elishama, Beeliada, and Eliphelet.

[8] When the Philistines heard that David had been anointed king over all Israel, they all went in search of David; when David heard of this, he went out to face them. [9] Now the Philistines had come and raided in Rephaim Valley, [10] so David inquired of God, "Should I attack the Philistines? Will you hand them over to me?"

The LORD replied, "Attack, and I will hand them over to you."

[11] So the Israelites went up to Baal-perazim, and David defeated the Philistines there. Then David said, "Like a bursting flood, God has used me to burst out against my enemies." Therefore, they named that place The Lord Bursts Out. [12] The Philistines abandoned their idols there, and David ordered that they be burned in the fire.

[13] Once again the Philistines raided in the valley. [14] So David again inquired of God, and God answered him, "Do not pursue them directly. Circle around them and attack them opposite the balsam trees. [15] When you hear the sound of marching in the tops of the balsam trees, then go out to battle, for God will have gone out ahead of you to strike down the army of the Philistines." [16] So David did as God commanded him, and they struck down the Philistine army from Gibeon to Gezer. [17] Then David's fame spread throughout the lands, and the LORD caused all the nations to be terrified of him.

🔖 GOING DEEPER

PSALM 21

The King's Victory

For the choir director. A psalm of David.

[1] LORD, the king finds joy in your strength.
How greatly he rejoices in your victory!

2 You have given him his heart's desire
and have not denied the request of his lips.   *Selah*
3 For you meet him with rich blessings;
you place a crown of pure gold on his head.
4 He asked you for life, and you gave it to him—
length of days forever and ever.
5 His glory is great through your victory;
you confer majesty and splendor on him.
6 You give him blessings forever;
you cheer him with joy in your presence.

7 For the king relies on the LORD;
through the faithful love of the Most High
he is not shaken.

8 Your hand will capture all your enemies;
your right hand will seize those who hate you.
9 You will make them burn
like a fiery furnace when you appear;
the LORD will engulf them in his wrath,
and fire will devour them.
10 You will wipe their progeny from the earth
and their offspring from the human race.
11 Though they intend to harm you
and devise a wicked plan, they will not prevail.
12 Instead, you will put them to flight
when you ready your bowstrings to shoot at them.

13 Be exalted, LORD, in your strength;
we will sing and praise your might.

Israel and Judah

The biblical account of the Israelites begins with the stories of Abraham, Isaac, and Jacob, who are often referred to as "the patriarchs." Their descendants were referred to as HEBREWS by other nations and people, most often before they entered the promised land (GN 14:13; EX 1:1–20). The ISRAELITES also used this term for themselves when talking with other people groups.

Jacob had twelve sons. The descendants of the twelve sons became known as the TRIBES OF ISRAEL, with each tribe bearing the name of either one of Jacob's sons or grandsons (GN 49:1–28). Israel's fourth son was named JUDAH. While those in the TRIBE OF JUDAH were also ISRAELITES, they more specifically could be referred to as JUDAHITES.

The words *Israel* and *Judah* occur hundreds of times in the Bible. Sometimes the terms refer to a person or group of people, an area of land, or a kingdom. This overview looks at the way each is used to reference Israel and Judah throughout Scripture. As you read 1 & 2 Chronicles or any other Old Testament book, use this point of reference to help guide you in understanding where the author is speaking about an individual tribe, kingdom, or the whole of God's old covenant people.

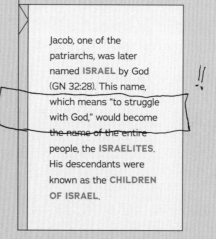

Jacob, one of the patriarchs, was later named ISRAEL by God (GN 32:28). This name, which means "to struggle with God," would become the name of the entire people, the ISRAELITES. His descendants were known as the CHILDREN OF ISRAEL.

The northern **TRIBES OF ISRAEL** were defeated and taken into exile by the Assyrians (2Kg 15:29; 17:6). After this, both **ISRAEL** and **JUDAH** were used to reference people from the two tribes that made up the southern kingdom, the only formal remaining group of God's people. Even after the southern kingdom of **JUDAH** was taken into exile by the Babylonians (Dn 1:1–4; 2Kg 24:10–17; 25:21; 2Ch 36:11–21), both **ISRAEL** and **JUDAH** were used to identify God's people.

Throughout the New Testament, those who descended from Jacob, no matter their tribe, were identified as **HEBREWS**, **ISRAELITES**, and **JUDEANS**.[1] The Israelite religion practiced by those who returned from exile became known as **JUDAISM**.

When Saul (who was from the tribe of Benjamin) and David and Solomon (who were from the **TRIBE OF JUDAH**) reigned, all twelve tribes were one, known as the **UNITED KINGDOM OF ISRAEL**.

When the tribes entered and conquered the promised land, the land became known as the **LAND OF ISRAEL** (JOS 11:23). Land was allocated to individual tribes and named after the tribe. The **LAND OF JUDAH** was a part of the **LAND OF ISRAEL**.

When the kingdom of **ISRAEL** split in a civil war in 931 BC (1KG 12:1–19), the ten **NORTHERN TRIBES OF ISRAEL** (also known as the **NORTHERN KINGDOM**) continued to be known as **ISRAEL**, and the tribes of **JUDAH** and Benjamin were identified as **JUDAH** (also known as the **SOUTHERN KINGDOM**). Jerusalem was the capital of the **SOUTHERN KINGDOM OF JUDAH**.

After the people were allowed to return to the land of the southern kingdom from Babylon, they were collectively known as **JUDAHITES**. The Greek name for the region of **JUDAH** was Judea (MT 2:1), and the people living there were called **JUDEANS**, as well as the land itself (MK 1:5).

---

[1] In the tenth and eleventh century, "**JUDEAN**" eventually became shortened to the first syllable, "Jew." (If you say both words out loud, you can hear the connection.) Many English Bibles translate the Hebrew word for **JUDAHITE** and the Greek word for **JUDEAN** as "Jew" in the Old and New Testaments.

GOD'S
PEOPLE
UNITED

DAY 10

WEEK 2

David Gives Thanks to the Lord

1 CHRONICLES 15

The Ark Comes to Jerusalem

¹ David built houses for himself in the city of David, and he prepared a place for the ark of God and pitched a tent for it. ² Then David said, "No one but the Levites may carry the ark of God, because the LORD has chosen them to carry the ark of the LORD and to minister before him forever."

³ David assembled all Israel at Jerusalem to bring the ark of the LORD to the place he had prepared for it. ⁴ Then he gathered together the descendants of Aaron and the Levites:

⁵ From the Kohathites, Uriel the leader and 120 of his relatives; ⁶ from the Merarites, Asaiah the leader and 220 of his relatives; ⁷ from the Gershomites, Joel the leader and 130 of his relatives; ⁸ from the Elizaphanites, Shemaiah the leader and 200 of his relatives; ⁹ from the Hebronites, Eliel the leader and 80 of his relatives; ¹⁰ from the Uzzielites, Amminadab the leader and 112 of his relatives.

¹¹ David summoned the priests Zadok and Abiathar and the Levites Uriel, Asaiah, Joel, Shemaiah, Eliel, and Amminadab. ¹² He said to them, "You are the heads of the Levite families. You and your relatives must consecrate yourselves so that you may bring the ark of the LORD God of Israel to the place I have prepared for it. ¹³ For the LORD our God burst out in anger against us because you Levites were not with us the first time, for we

didn't inquire of him about the proper procedures." [14] So the priests and the Levites consecrated themselves to bring up the ark of the LORD God of Israel. [15] Then the Levites carried the ark of God the way Moses had commanded according to the word of the LORD: on their shoulders with the poles.

[16] Then David told the leaders of the Levites to appoint their relatives as singers and to have them raise their voices with joy accompanied by musical instruments—harps, lyres, and cymbals. [17] So the Levites appointed Heman son of Joel; from his relatives, Asaph son of Berechiah; and from their relatives the Merarites, Ethan son of Kushaiah. [18] With them were their relatives second in rank: Zechariah, Jaaziel, Shemiramoth, Jehiel, Unni, Eliab, Benaiah, Maaseiah, Mattithiah, Eliphelehu, Mikneiah, and the gatekeepers Obed-edom and Jeiel. [19] The singers Heman, Asaph, and Ethan were to sound the bronze cymbals; [20] Zechariah, Aziel, Shemiramoth, Jehiel, Unni, Eliab, Maaseiah, and Benaiah were to play harps according to *Alamoth* [21] and Mattithiah, Eliphelehu, Mikneiah, Obed-edom, Jeiel, and Azaziah were to lead the music with lyres according to the *Sheminith*. [22] Chenaniah, the leader of the Levites in music, was to direct the music because he was skillful. [23] Berechiah and Elkanah were to be gatekeepers for the ark. [24] The priests, Shebaniah, Joshaphat, Nethanel, Amasai, Zechariah, Benaiah, and Eliezer, were to blow trumpets before the ark of God. Obed-edom and Jehiah were also to be gatekeepers for the ark.

[25] David, the elders of Israel, and the commanders of thousands went with rejoicing to bring the ark of the covenant of the LORD from the house of Obed-edom. [26] Because God helped the Levites who were carrying the ark of the covenant of the LORD, with God's help, they sacrificed seven bulls and seven rams.

[27] Now David was dressed in a robe of fine linen, as were all the Levites who were carrying the ark, as well as the singers and Chenaniah, the music leader of the singers. David also wore a linen ephod. [28] So all Israel brought up the ark of the covenant of the LORD with shouts, the sound of the ram's horn, trumpets, and cymbals, and the playing of harps and lyres. [29] As the ark of the covenant of the LORD was entering the city of David, Saul's daughter Michal looked down from the window and saw King David leaping and dancing, and she despised him in her heart.

1 CHRONICLES 16

[1] They brought the ark of God and placed it inside the tent David had pitched for it. Then they offered burnt offerings and fellowship offerings in God's presence. [2] When David had finished offering the burnt offerings and the fellowship offerings, he blessed the people in the name of the LORD. [3] Then he distributed to each and every Israelite, both men and women, a loaf of bread, a date cake, and a raisin cake.

[4] David appointed some of the Levites to be ministers before the ark of the LORD, to celebrate the LORD God of Israel, and to give thanks and praise to him. [5] Asaph was the chief and Zechariah was second to him. Jeiel, Shemiramoth, Jehiel, Mattithiah, Eliab, Benaiah, Obed-edom, and Jeiel played the harps and lyres, while Asaph sounded the cymbals [6] and the priests Benaiah and Jahaziel blew the trumpets regularly before the ark of the covenant of God.

David's Psalm of Thanksgiving

[7] On that day David decreed for the first time that thanks be given to the LORD by Asaph and his relatives:

[8] Give thanks to the LORD; call on his name;
proclaim his deeds among the peoples.
[9] Sing to him; sing praise to him;
tell about all his wondrous works!
[10] Boast in his holy name;
let the hearts of those who seek the LORD rejoice.
[11] Seek the LORD and his strength;
seek his face always.
[12] Remember the wondrous works he has done,
his wonders, and the judgments he has pronounced,
[13] you offspring of Israel his servant,
Jacob's descendants—his chosen ones.

[14] He is the LORD our God;
his judgments govern the whole earth.

¹⁵ Remember his covenant forever—
the promise he ordained for a thousand generations,
¹⁶ the covenant he made with Abraham,
swore to Isaac,
¹⁷ and confirmed to Jacob as a decree,
and to Israel as a permanent covenant:
¹⁸ "I will give the land of Canaan to you
as your inherited portion."

¹⁹ When they were few in number,
very few indeed, and resident aliens in Canaan
²⁰ wandering from nation to nation
and from one kingdom to another,
²¹ he allowed no one to oppress them;
he rebuked kings on their behalf:
²² "Do not touch my anointed ones
or harm my prophets."

²³ Let the whole earth sing to the LORD.
Proclaim his salvation from day to day.
²⁴ Declare his glory among the nations,
his wondrous works among all peoples.

²⁵ For the LORD is great and highly praised;
he is feared above all gods.
²⁶ For all the gods of the peoples are worthless idols,
but the LORD made the heavens.
²⁷ Splendor and majesty are before him;
strength and joy are in his place.
²⁸ Ascribe to the LORD, families of the peoples,
ascribe to the LORD glory and strength.
²⁹ Ascribe to the LORD the glory of his name;
bring an offering and come before him.
Worship the LORD in the splendor of his holiness;
³⁰ let the whole earth tremble before him.
The world is firmly established;
it cannot be shaken.
³¹ Let the heavens be glad and the earth rejoice,
and let them say among the nations, "The LORD reigns!"
³² Let the sea and all that fills it resound;
let the fields and everything in them exult.
³³ Then the trees of the forest will shout for joy before

the LORD,
for he is coming to judge the earth.

³⁴ Give thanks to the LORD, for he is good;
his faithful love endures forever.
³⁵ And say, "Save us, God of our salvation;
gather us and rescue us from the nations
so that we may give thanks to your holy name
and rejoice in your praise.
³⁶ Blessed be the LORD God of Israel
from everlasting to everlasting."

Then all the people said, "Amen" and "Praise the LORD."

³⁷ So David left Asaph and his relatives there before the ark of the LORD's covenant to minister regularly before the ark according to the daily requirements. ³⁸ He assigned Obed-edom and his sixty-eight relatives. Obed-edom son of Jeduthun and Hosah were to be gatekeepers. ³⁹ David left the priest Zadok and his fellow priests before the tabernacle of the LORD at the high place in Gibeon ⁴⁰ to offer burnt offerings regularly, morning and evening, to the LORD on the altar of burnt offerings and to do everything that was written in the law of the LORD, which he had commanded Israel to keep. ⁴¹ With them were Heman, Jeduthun, and the rest who were chosen and designated by name to give thanks to the LORD—for his faithful love endures forever. ⁴² Heman and Jeduthun had with them trumpets and cymbals to play and musical instruments of God. Jeduthun's sons were at the city gate.

⁴³ Then all the people went home, and David returned home to bless his household.

◗ GOING DEEPER

HEBREWS 13:15

Therefore, through him let us continually offer up to God a sacrifice of praise, that is, the fruit of lips that confess his name.

GOD'S
PEOPLE
UNITED

The Lord's Covenant with David

DAY 11

WEEK 2

1 CHRONICLES 17

The LORD's Covenant with David

¹ When David had settled into his palace, he said to the prophet Nathan, "Look! I am living in a cedar house while the ark of the LORD's covenant is under tent curtains."

² So Nathan told David, "Do all that is on your mind, for God is with you."

³ But that night the word of God came to Nathan: ⁴ "Go to David my servant and say, 'This is what the LORD says: You are not the one to build me a house to dwell in. ⁵ From the time I brought Israel out of Egypt until today I have not dwelt in a house; instead, I have moved from one tent site to another, and from one tabernacle location to another. ⁶ In all my journeys throughout Israel, have I ever spoken a word to even one of the judges of Israel, whom I commanded to shepherd my people, asking: Why haven't you built me a house of cedar?'

⁷ "So now this is what you are to say to my servant David: 'This is what the LORD of Armies says: I took you from the pasture, from tending the flock, to be ruler over my people Israel. ⁸ I have been with you wherever you have gone, and I have destroyed all your enemies before you. I will make a name for you like that of the greatest on the earth. ⁹ I will designate a place for my people Israel and plant them, so that they may live there and not be disturbed again. Evildoers will not continue to oppress them as they have done ¹⁰ ever since the day I ordered judges to be over my people Israel. I will also subdue all your enemies.

"'Furthermore, I declare to you that the LORD himself will build a house for you. ¹¹ When your time comes to be with your ancestors, I will raise up after you your descendant, who is one of your own sons, and I will establish his kingdom. ¹² He is the one who will build a house for me, and I will establish his throne forever. [13] I will be his father, and he will be my son. I will not remove my faithful love from him as I removed it from the one who was before you.

[14] I will appoint him over my house and my kingdom forever, and his throne will be established forever.'"

[15] Nathan reported all these words and this entire vision to David.

David's Prayer of Thanksgiving

[16] Then King David went in, sat in the LORD's presence, and said,

Who am I, LORD God, and what is my house that you have brought me this far? [17] This was a little thing to you, God, for you have spoken about your servant's house in the distant future. You regard me as a man of distinction, LORD God. [18] What more can David say to you for honoring your servant? You know your servant. [19] LORD, you have done this whole great thing, making known all these great promises for the sake of your servant and according to your will. [20] LORD, there is no one like you, and there is no God besides you, as all we have heard confirms. [21] And who is like your people Israel? God, you came to one nation on earth to redeem a people for yourself, to make a name for yourself through great and awesome works by driving out nations before your people you redeemed from Egypt. [22] You made your people Israel your own people forever, and you, LORD, have become their God.

[23] Now, LORD, let the word that you have spoken concerning your servant and his house be confirmed forever, and do as you have promised. [24] Let your name be confirmed and magnified forever in the saying, "The LORD of Armies, the God of Israel, is God over Israel." May the house of your servant David be established before you. [25] Since you, my God, have revealed to your servant that you will build him a house, your servant has found courage to pray in your presence. [26] LORD, you indeed are God, and you have promised this good thing to your servant. [27] So now, you have been pleased to bless your servant's house that it may continue before you forever. For you, LORD, have blessed it, and it is blessed forever.

ROMANS 1:1-6

The Gospel of God for Rome

[1] Paul, a servant of Christ Jesus, called as an apostle and set apart for the gospel of God— [2] which he promised beforehand through his prophets in the Holy Scriptures— [3] concerning his Son, Jesus Christ our Lord, who was a descendant of David according to the flesh [4] and was appointed to be the powerful Son of God according to the Spirit of holiness by the resurrection of the dead. [5] Through him we have received grace and apostleship to bring about the obedience of faith for the sake of his name among all the Gentiles, [6] including you who are also called by Jesus Christ.

David's Military Campaigns

DAY 12

WEEK 2

1 CHRONICLES 18

David's Military Campaigns

¹ After this, David defeated the Philistines, subdued them, and took Gath and its surrounding villages from Philistine control. ² He also defeated the Moabites, and they became David's subjects and brought tribute.

³ David also defeated King Hadadezer of Zobah at Hamath when he went to establish his control at the Euphrates River. ⁴ David captured one thousand chariots, seven thousand horsemen, and twenty thousand foot soldiers from him, hamstrung all the horses, and kept a hundred chariots.

⁵ When the Arameans of Damascus came to assist King Hadadezer of Zobah, David struck down twenty-two thousand Aramean men. ⁶ Then he placed garrisons in Aram of Damascus, and the Arameans became David's subjects and brought tribute. The LORD made David victorious wherever he went.

⁷ David took the gold shields carried by Hadadezer's officers and brought them to Jerusalem. ⁸ From Tibhath and Cun, Hadadezer's cities, David also took huge quantities of bronze, from which Solomon made the bronze basin, the pillars, and the bronze articles.

⁹ When King Tou of Hamath heard that David had defeated the entire army of King Hadadezer of Zobah, ¹⁰ he sent his son Hadoram to King David to greet him and to congratulate him because David had fought against Hadadezer and defeated him, for Tou and Hadadezer had fought many wars. Hadoram brought all kinds of gold, silver, and bronze items. ¹¹ King David also dedicated these to the LORD, along with the silver and gold he had carried off from all the nations—from Edom, Moab, the Ammonites, the Philistines, and the Amalekites.

¹² Abishai son of Zeruiah struck down eighteen thousand Edomites in the Salt Valley. ¹³ He put garrisons in Edom, and all the Edomites were subject to David. The LORD made David victorious wherever he went.

¹⁴ So David reigned over all Israel, administering justice and righteousness for all his people.

¹⁵ Joab son of Zeruiah was over the army;
Jehoshaphat son of Ahilud was court historian;
¹⁶ Zadok son of Ahitub and Ahimelech son of Abiathar were priests;
Shavsha was court secretary;
¹⁷ Benaiah son of Jehoiada was over the Cherethites and the Pelethites;
and David's sons were the chief officials at the king's side.

1 CHRONICLES 19

War with the Ammonites

¹ Some time later, King Nahash of the Ammonites died, and his son became king in his place. ² Then David said, "I'll show kindness to Hanun son of Nahash, because his father showed kindness to me."

So David sent messengers to console him concerning his father. However, when David's emissaries arrived in the land of the Ammonites to console him, ³ the Ammonite leaders said to Hanun, "Just because David has sent men with condolences for you, do you really believe he's showing respect for your father? Instead, haven't his emissaries come in order to scout out, overthrow, and spy on the land?" ⁴ So Hanun took David's emissaries, shaved them, cut their clothes in half at the hips, and sent them away.

⁵ It was reported to David about his men, so he sent messengers to meet them, since the men were deeply humiliated. The king said, "Stay in Jericho until your beards grow back; then return."

⁶ When the Ammonites realized they had made themselves repulsive to David, Hanun and the Ammonites sent thirty-eight tons of silver to hire chariots and horsemen from Aram-naharaim, Aram-maacah, and Zobah. ⁷ They hired thirty-two thousand chariots and the king of Maacah with his army, who came and camped near Medeba. The Ammonites also came together from their cities for the battle.

⁸ David heard about this and sent Joab and all the elite troops. ⁹ The Ammonites marched out and lined up in battle formation at the entrance of the city while the kings who had come were in the field by themselves. ¹⁰ When Joab saw that there was a battle line in front of him and another behind him, he chose some of Israel's finest young men and lined up in formation to engage the Arameans. ¹¹ He placed the rest of the forces under the command of his brother Abishai. They lined up in formation to engage the Ammonites.

¹² "If the Arameans are too strong for me," Joab said, "then you'll be my help. However, if the Ammonites are too strong for you, I'll help you.

¹³ Be strong! Let's prove ourselves strong for our people and for the cities of our God. May the LORD's will be done."

¹⁴ Joab and the people with him approached the Arameans for battle, and they fled before him. ¹⁵ When the Ammonites saw that the Arameans had fled, they likewise fled before Joab's brother Abishai and entered the city. Then Joab went to Jerusalem.

¹⁶ When the Arameans realized that they had been defeated by Israel, they sent messengers to summon the Arameans who were beyond the Euphrates River. They were led by Shophach, the commander of Hadadezer's army.

¹⁷ When this was reported to David, he gathered all Israel and crossed the Jordan. He came up to the Arameans and lined up against them. When David lined up to engage them, they fought against him. ¹⁸ But the Arameans fled before Israel, and David killed seven thousand of their charioteers and forty thousand foot soldiers. He also killed Shophach, commander of the army. ¹⁹ When Hadadezer's subjects saw that they had been defeated by Israel, they made peace with David and became his subjects. After this, the Arameans were never willing to help the Ammonites again.

1 CHRONICLES 20

Capture of the City of Rabbah

¹ In the spring when kings march out to war, Joab led the army and destroyed the Ammonites' land. He came to Rabbah and besieged it, but David remained in Jerusalem. Joab attacked Rabbah and demolished it. ² Then David took the crown from the head of their king, and it was placed on

David's head. He found that the crown weighed seventy-five pounds of gold, and there was a precious stone in it. In addition, David took away a large quantity of plunder from the city. ³ He brought out the people who were in it and put them to work with saws, iron picks, and axes. David did the same to all the Ammonite cities. Then he and all his troops returned to Jerusalem.

The Philistine Giants

⁴ After this, a war broke out with the Philistines at Gezer. At that time Sibbecai the Hushathite killed Sippai, a descendant of the Rephaim, and the Philistines were subdued.

⁵ Once again there was a battle with the Philistines, and Elhanan son of Jair killed Lahmi the brother of Goliath of Gath. The shaft of his spear was like a weaver's beam.

⁶ There was still another battle at Gath where there was a man of extraordinary stature with six fingers on each hand and six toes on each foot—twenty-four in all. He, too, was descended from the giant. ⁷ When he taunted Israel, Jonathan son of David's brother Shimei killed him.

⁸ These were the descendants of the giant in Gath killed by David and his soldiers.

■ GOING DEEPER

PSALM 110:1-3

The Priestly King
A psalm of David.

¹ This is the declaration of the LORD
to my Lord:
"Sit at my right hand
until I make your enemies your footstool."
² The LORD will extend your mighty scepter from Zion.
Rule over your surrounding enemies.
³ Your people will volunteer
on your day of battle.
In holy splendor, from the womb of the dawn,
the dew of your youth belongs to you.

HYMN

Crown Him with Many Crowns

WORDS: Stanzas 1, 3, and 4 by Matthew Bridges; stanza 2 by Godfrey Thring
MUSIC: George J. Elvey; last stanza setting and choral ending by David Winkler

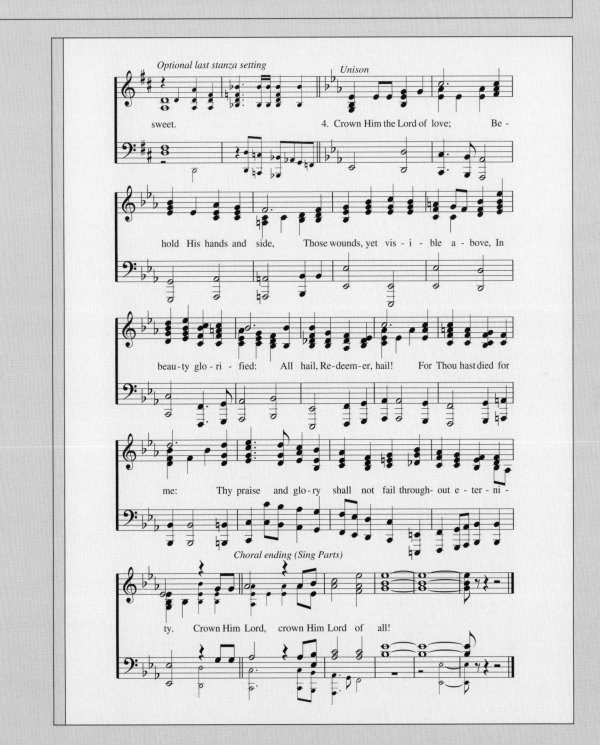

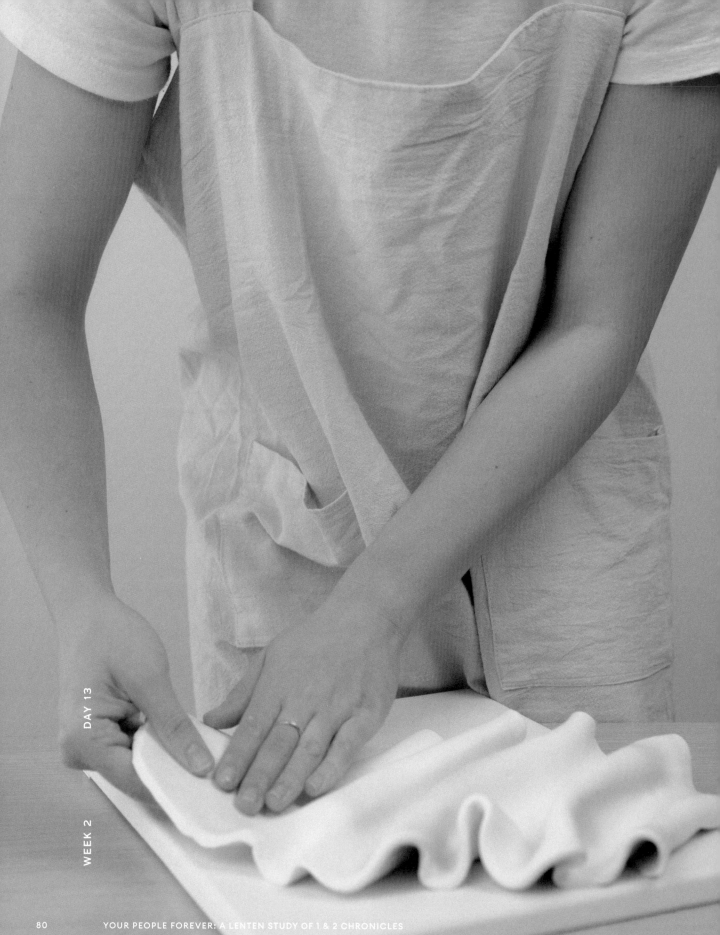

Grace Day

Therefore, through him let us continually offer up to God a sacrifice of praise, that is, the fruit of lips that confess his name.

Take this day to catch up on your reading, pray, and rest in the presence of the Lord.

HEBREWS 13:15

Weekly Truth

Scripture is God-breathed and true. When we memorize it, we carry His Word with us wherever we go.

During this reading plan, we are working to memorize 1 Chronicles 29:11–13. This week we will add the rest of verse 11, remembering that the kingdom belongs to the Lord.

See tips for memorizing Scripture on page 240.

Yours, LORD, is the greatness and the power and the glory and the splendor and the majesty, for everything in the heavens and on earth belongs to you. Yours, LORD, is the kingdom, and you are exalted as head over all. Riches and honor come from you, and you are the ruler of everything. Power and might are in your hand, and it is in your hand to make great and to give strength to all. Now therefore, our God, we give you thanks and praise your glorious name.

1 CHRONICLES 29:11-13

DAY 15

WEEK 3

Preparations
for the Temple

1 CHRONICLES 21

David's Military Census

¹ Satan rose up against Israel and incited David to count the people of Israel. ² So David said to Joab and the commanders of the troops, "Go and count Israel from Beer-sheba to Dan and bring a report to me so I can know their number."

³ Joab replied, "May the LORD multiply the number of his people a hundred times over! My lord the king, aren't they all my lord's servants? Why does my lord want to do this? Why should he bring guilt on Israel?"

⁴ Yet the king's order prevailed over Joab. So Joab left and traveled throughout Israel and then returned to Jerusalem. ⁵ Joab gave the total troop registration to David. In all Israel there were one million one hundred thousand armed men and in Judah itself four hundred seventy thousand armed men. ⁶ But he did not include Levi and Benjamin in the count because the king's command was detestable to him. ⁷ This command was also evil in God's sight, so he afflicted Israel.

⁸ David said to God, "I have sinned greatly because I have done this thing. Now, please take away your servant's guilt, for I've been very foolish."

David's Punishment

⁹ Then the Lord instructed Gad, David's seer, ¹⁰ "Go and say to David, 'This is what the Lord says: I am offering you three choices. Choose one of them for yourself, and I will do it to you.'"

¹¹ So Gad went to David and said to him, "This is what the Lord says: 'Take your choice: ¹² three years of famine, or three months of devastation by your foes with the sword of your enemy overtaking you, or three days of the sword of the Lord—a plague on the land, the angel of the Lord bringing destruction to the whole territory of Israel.' Now decide what answer I should take back to the one who sent me."

¹³ David answered Gad, "I'm in anguish. Please, let me fall into the Lord's hands because his mercies are very great, but don't let me fall into human hands."

¹⁴ So the Lord sent a plague on Israel, and seventy thousand Israelite men died. ¹⁵ Then God sent an angel to Jerusalem to destroy it, but when the angel was about to destroy the city, the Lord looked, relented concerning the destruction, and said to the angel who was destroying the people, "Enough, withdraw your hand now!" The angel of the Lord was then standing at the threshing floor of Ornan the Jebusite.

¹⁶ When David looked up and saw the angel of the Lord standing between earth and heaven, with his drawn sword in his hand stretched out over Jerusalem, David and the elders, covered in sackcloth, fell facedown. ¹⁷ David said to God, "Wasn't I the one who gave the order to count the people? I am the one who has sinned and acted very wickedly. But these sheep, what have they done? Lord my God, please let your hand be against me and against my father's family, but don't let the plague be against your people."

David's Altar

¹⁸ So the angel of the Lord ordered Gad to tell David to go and set up an altar to the Lord on the threshing floor of Ornan the Jebusite. ¹⁹ David went up at Gad's command spoken in the name of the Lord.

²⁰ Ornan was threshing wheat when he turned and saw the angel. His four sons, who were with him, hid. ²¹ David came to Ornan, and when Ornan looked and saw David, he left the threshing floor and bowed to David with his face to the ground.

²² Then David said to Ornan, "Give me this threshing-floor plot so that I may build an altar to the Lord on it. Give it to me for the full price, so the plague on the people may be stopped."

²³ Ornan said to David, "Take it! My lord the king may do whatever he wants. See, I give the oxen for the burnt offerings, the threshing sledges for the wood, and the wheat for the grain offering—I give it all."

²⁴ King David answered Ornan, "No, I insist on paying the full price, for I will not take for the Lord what belongs to you or offer burnt offerings that cost me nothing."

²⁵ So David gave Ornan fifteen pounds of gold for the plot. ²⁶ He built an altar to the Lord there and offered burnt offerings and fellowship offerings. He called on the Lord, and he answered him with fire from heaven on the altar of burnt offering.

²⁷ Then the Lord spoke to the angel, and he put his sword back into its sheath. ²⁸ At that time, David offered sacrifices there when he saw that the Lord answered him at the threshing floor of Ornan the Jebusite. ²⁹ The tabernacle of the Lord, which Moses made in the wilderness, and the altar of burnt offering were at the high place in Gibeon, ³⁰ but David could not go before it to inquire of God, because he was terrified of the sword of the Lord's angel.

1 CHRONICLES 22

¹ Then David said, "This is the house of the Lord God, and this is the altar of burnt offering for Israel."

David's Preparations for the Temple

² So David gave orders to gather the resident aliens that were in the land of Israel, and he appointed stonecutters to cut finished stones for building God's house. ³ David supplied a great deal of iron to make the nails for the doors of the gates and for the fittings, together with an immeasurable quantity of bronze, ⁴ and innumerable cedar logs because the Sidonians and Tyrians had brought a large quantity of cedar logs to David. ⁵ David said, "My son Solomon is young and inexperienced, and the house that is to be built for the LORD must be exceedingly great and famous and glorious in all the lands. Therefore, I will make provision for it." So David made lavish preparations for it before his death.

⁶ Then he summoned his son Solomon and charged him to build a house for the LORD God of Israel. ⁷ "My son," David said to Solomon, "It was in my heart to build a house for the name of the LORD my God, ⁸ but the word of the LORD came to me: 'You have shed much blood and waged great wars. You are not to build a house for my name because you have shed so much blood on the ground before me. ⁹ But a son will be born to you; he will be a man of rest. I will give him rest from all his surrounding enemies, for his name will be Solomon, and I will give peace and quiet to Israel during his reign. ¹⁰ He is the one who will build a house for my name. He will be my son, and I will be his father. I will establish the throne of his kingdom over Israel forever.'

¹¹ "Now, my son, may the LORD be with you, and may you succeed in building the house of the LORD your God, as he said about you.

¹² Above all, may the LORD give you insight and understanding when he puts you in charge of Israel so that you may keep the law of the LORD your God. ¹³ Then you will succeed if you carefully follow the statutes and ordinances the LORD commanded Moses for Israel. Be strong and courageous. Don't be afraid or discouraged.

¹⁴ "Notice I have taken great pains to provide for the house of the LORD—3,775 tons of gold, 37,750 tons of silver, and bronze and iron that can't be weighed because there is so much of it. I have also provided timber and stone, but you will need to add more to them. ¹⁵ You also have many workers: stonecutters, masons, carpenters, and people skilled in every kind of work ¹⁶ in gold, silver, bronze, and iron—beyond number. Now begin the work, and may the LORD be with you."

¹⁷ Then David ordered all the leaders of Israel to help his son Solomon: ¹⁸ "The LORD your God is with you, isn't he? And hasn't he given you rest on every side? For he has handed the land's inhabitants over to me, and the land has been subdued before the LORD and his people. ¹⁹ Now determine in your mind and heart to seek the LORD your God. Get started building the LORD God's sanctuary so that you may bring the ark of the LORD's covenant and the holy articles of God to the temple that is to be built for the name of the LORD."

◗ GOING DEEPER

DEUTERONOMY 12:1–5

The Chosen Place of Worship

¹ Be careful to follow these statutes and ordinances in the land that the LORD, the God of your ancestors, has given you to possess all the days you live on the earth. ² Destroy completely all the places where the nations that you are driving out worship their gods—on the high mountains, on the hills, and under every green tree. ³ Tear down their altars, smash their sacred pillars, burn their Asherah poles, cut down the carved images of their gods, and wipe out their names from every place. ⁴ Don't worship the LORD your God this way. ⁵ Instead, turn to the place the LORD your God chooses from all your tribes to put his name for his dwelling and go there.

The Divisions of the Levites

1 CHRONICLES 23

The Divisions of the Levites

¹ When David was old and full of days, he installed his son Solomon as king over Israel. ² Then he gathered all the leaders of Israel, the priests, and the Levites. ³ The Levites thirty years old or more were counted; the total number of men was thirty-eight thousand by headcount. ⁴ "Of these," David said, "twenty-four thousand are to be in charge of the work on the LORD's temple, six thousand are to be officers and judges, ⁵ four thousand are to be gatekeepers, and four thousand are to praise the LORD with the instruments that I have made for worship."

⁶ Then David divided them into divisions according to Levi's sons: Gershom, Kohath, and Merari.

⁷ The Gershonites: Ladan and Shimei.
⁸ Ladan's sons: Jehiel was the first, then Zetham, and Joel—three.
⁹ Shimei's sons: Shelomoth, Haziel, and Haran—three. Those were the heads of the families of Ladan.

¹⁰ Shimei's sons: Jahath, Zizah, Jeush, and Beriah. Those were Shimei's sons—four. ¹¹ Jahath was the first and Zizah was the second; however, Jeush and Beriah did not have many sons, so they became one family and received a single assignment.

¹² Kohath's sons: Amram, Izhar, Hebron, and Uzziel—four.

¹³ Amram's sons: Aaron and Moses.

Aaron, along with his descendants, was set apart forever to consecrate the most holy things, to burn incense in the presence of the LORD, to minister to him, and to pronounce blessings in his name forever. ¹⁴ As for Moses the man of God, his sons were named among the tribe of Levi.

¹⁵ Moses's sons: Gershom and Eliezer.

¹⁶ Gershom's sons: Shebuel was first.

¹⁷ Eliezer's sons were Rehabiah, first; Eliezer did not have any other sons, but Rehabiah's sons were very numerous.

¹⁸ Izhar's sons: Shelomith was first.

¹⁹ Hebron's sons: Jeriah was first, Amariah second, Jahaziel third, and Jekameam fourth.

²⁰ Uzziel's sons: Micah was first, and Isshiah second.

²¹ Merari's sons: Mahli and Mushi.

Mahli's sons: Eleazar and Kish.

²² Eleazar died having no sons, only daughters. Their cousins, the sons of Kish, married them.

²³ Mushi's sons: Mahli, Eder, and Jeremoth—three.

²⁴ These were the descendants of Levi by their ancestral families—the family heads, according to their registration by name in the headcount—twenty years old or more, who worked in the service of the LORD's temple. ²⁵ For David said, "The LORD God of Israel has given rest to his people, and he has come to stay in Jerusalem forever. ²⁶ Also, the Levites no longer need to carry the tabernacle or any of the equipment for its service"— ²⁷ for according to the last words of David, the Levites twenty years old or more were to be counted—

²⁸ "but their duty will be to assist the descendants of Aaron with the service of the LORD's temple, being responsible for the courts and the chambers, the purification of all the holy things, and the work of the service of God's temple—

²⁹ as well as the rows of the Bread of the Presence, the fine flour for the grain offering, the wafers of unleavened bread, the baking, the mixing, and all measurements of volume and length. ³⁰ They are also to stand every morning to give thanks and praise to the LORD, and likewise in the evening. ³¹ Whenever burnt offerings are offered to the LORD on the Sabbaths, New Moons, and appointed festivals, they are to offer them regularly in the LORD's presence according to the number prescribed for them. ³² They are to carry out their responsibilities for the tent of meeting, for the holy place, and for their relatives, the descendants of Aaron, in the service of the LORD's temple."

1 CHRONICLES 24

The Divisions of the Priests

¹ The divisions of the descendants of Aaron were as follows: Aaron's sons were Nadab, Abihu, Eleazar, and Ithamar. ² But Nadab and Abihu died before their father, and they had no sons, so Eleazar and Ithamar served as priests. ³ Together with Zadok from the descendants of Eleazar and Ahimelech from

the descendants of Ithamar, David divided them according to the assigned duties of their service. [4] Since more leaders were found among Eleazar's descendants than Ithamar's, they were divided accordingly: sixteen heads of ancestral families were from Eleazar's descendants, and eight heads of ancestral families were from Ithamar's. [5] They were assigned by lot, for there were officers of the sanctuary and officers of God among both Eleazar's and Ithamar's descendants.

[6] The secretary, Shemaiah son of Nethanel, a Levite, recorded them in the presence of the king and the officers, the priest Zadok, Ahimelech son of Abiathar, and the heads of families of the priests and the Levites. One ancestral family was taken for Eleazar, and then one for Ithamar.

[7] The first lot fell to Jehoiarib, the second to Jedaiah,
[8] the third to Harim, the fourth to Seorim,
[9] the fifth to Malchijah, the sixth to Mijamin,
[10] the seventh to Hakkoz, the eighth to Abijah,
[11] the ninth to Jeshua, the tenth to Shecaniah,
[12] the eleventh to Eliashib, the twelfth to Jakim,
[13] the thirteenth to Huppah, the fourteenth to Jeshebeab,
[14] the fifteenth to Bilgah, the sixteenth to Immer,
[15] the seventeenth to Hezir, the eighteenth to Happizzez,
[16] the nineteenth to Pethahiah, the twentieth to Jehezkel,
[17] the twenty-first to Jachin, the twenty-second to Gamul,
[18] the twenty-third to Delaiah, and the twenty-fourth to Maaziah.

[19] These had their assigned duties for service when they entered the Lord's temple, according to their regulations, which they received from their ancestor Aaron, as the Lord God of Israel had commanded him.

The Rest of the Levites

[20] As for the rest of Levi's sons:
from Amram's sons: Shubael;
from Shubael's sons: Jehdeiah.
[21] From Rehabiah:
from Rehabiah's sons: Isshiah was the first.
[22] From the Izharites: Shelomoth;
from Shelomoth's sons: Jahath.
[23] Hebron's sons:
Jeriah the first, Amariah the second,

Jahaziel the third, and Jekameam the fourth.
[24] From Uzziel's sons: Micah;
from Micah's sons: Shamir.
[25] Micah's brother: Isshiah;
from Isshiah's sons: Zechariah.
[26] Merari's sons: Mahli and Mushi,
and from his sons, Jaaziah his son.
[27] Merari's sons, by his son Jaaziah:
Shoham, Zaccur, and Ibri.
[28] From Mahli: Eleazar, who had no sons.
[29] From Kish, from Kish's sons: Jerahmeel.
[30] Mushi's sons: Mahli, Eder, and Jerimoth.

Those were the descendants of the Levites according to their ancestral families. [31] They also cast lots the same way as their relatives the descendants of Aaron did in the presence of King David, Zadok, Ahimelech, and the heads of the families of the priests and Levites—the family heads and their younger brothers alike.

1 CHRONICLES 25

The Levitical Musicians

[1] David and the officers of the army also set apart some of the sons of Asaph, Heman, and Jeduthun, who were to prophesy accompanied by lyres, harps, and cymbals. This is the list of the men who performed their service:

[2] From Asaph's sons:
Zaccur, Joseph, Nethaniah, and Asarelah, sons of Asaph, under Asaph's authority, who prophesied under the authority of the king.
[3] From Jeduthun: Jeduthun's sons:
Gedaliah, Zeri, Jeshaiah, Shimei, Hashabiah, and Mattithiah—six—under the authority of their father Jeduthun, prophesying to the accompaniment of lyres, giving thanks and praise to the Lord.
[4] From Heman: Heman's sons:
Bukkiah, Mattaniah, Uzziel, Shebuel, Jerimoth, Hananiah, Hanani, Eliathah, Giddalti, Romamti-ezer, Joshbekashah, Mallothi, Hothir, and Mahazioth. [5] All these sons of Heman, the king's seer, were given by the promises of God to exalt him, for God had given Heman fourteen sons and three daughters.

[6] All these men were under their own fathers' authority for the music in the LORD's temple, with cymbals, harps, and lyres for the service of God's temple. Asaph, Jeduthun, and Heman were under the king's authority. [7] They numbered 288 together with their relatives who were all trained and skillful in music for the LORD. [8] They cast lots for their duties, young and old alike, teacher as well as pupil.

[9] The first lot for Asaph fell to Joseph, his sons, and his relatives—	12
to Gedaliah the second: him, his relatives, and his sons—	12
[10] the third to Zaccur, his sons, and his relatives—	12
[11] the fourth to Izri, his sons, and his relatives—	12
[12] the fifth to Nethaniah, his sons, and his relatives—	12
[13] the sixth to Bukkiah, his sons, and his relatives—	12
[14] the seventh to Jesarelah, his sons, and his relatives—	12
[15] the eighth to Jeshaiah, his sons, and his relatives—	12
[16] the ninth to Mattaniah, his sons, and his relatives—	12
[17] the tenth to Shimei, his sons, and his relatives—	12
[18] the eleventh to Azarel, his sons, and his relatives—	12
[19] the twelfth to Hashabiah, his sons, and his relatives—	12
[20] the thirteenth to Shubael, his sons, and his relatives—	12
[21] the fourteenth to Mattithiah, his sons, and his relatives—	12
[22] the fifteenth to Jeremoth, his sons, and his relatives—	12
[23] the sixteenth to Hananiah, his sons, and his relatives—	12
[24] the seventeenth to Joshbekashah, his sons, and his relatives—	12
[25] the eighteenth to Hanani, his sons, and his relatives—	12
[26] the nineteenth to Mallothi, his sons, and his relatives—	12
[27] the twentieth to Eliathah, his sons, and his relatives—	12
[28] the twenty-first to Hothir, his sons, and his relatives—	12
[29] the twenty-second to Giddalti, his sons, and his relatives—	12
[30] the twenty-third to Mahazioth, his sons, and his relatives—	12
[31] and the twenty-fourth to Romamti-ezer, his sons, and his relatives—	12.

◖ GOING DEEPER

ROMANS 12:1

Therefore, brothers and sisters, in view of the mercies of God, I urge you to present your bodies as a living sacrifice, holy and pleasing to God; this is your true worship.

GOD'S
PEOPLE
UNITED

WEEK 3   DAY 17

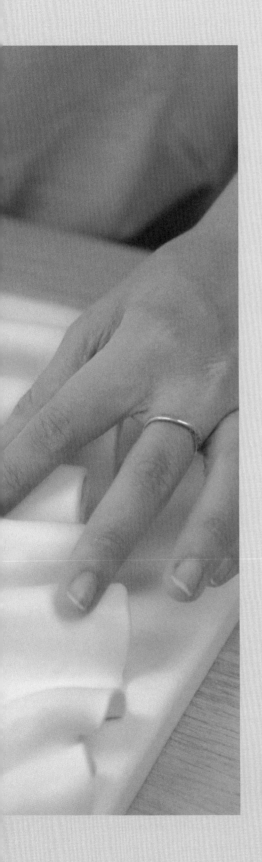

The Levitical Gatekeepers

1 CHRONICLES 26

The Levitical Gatekeepers

¹ The following were the divisions of the gatekeepers:

From the Korahites: Meshelemiah son of Kore, one of the sons of Asaph.
² Meshelemiah had sons:
Zechariah the firstborn, Jediael the second,
Zebadiah the third, Jathniel the fourth,
³ Elam the fifth, Jehohanan the sixth,
and Eliehoenai the seventh.
⁴ Obed-edom also had sons:
Shemaiah the firstborn, Jehozabad the second,
Joah the third, Sachar the fourth,
Nethanel the fifth, ⁵ Ammiel the sixth,
Issachar the seventh, and Peullethai the eighth,
for God blessed him.
⁶ Also, to his son Shemaiah were born sons who ruled their ancestral families because they were strong, capable men.
⁷ Shemaiah's sons: Othni, Rephael, Obed, and Elzabad; his relatives Elihu and Semachiah were also capable men. ⁸ All of these were among the sons of Obed-edom with their sons and relatives; they were capable men with strength for the work—sixty-two from Obed-edom.
⁹ Meshelemiah also had sons and relatives who were capable men—eighteen.
¹⁰ Hosah, from the Merarites, also had sons: Shimri the first (although he was not the firstborn, his father had appointed

him as the first), [11] Hilkiah the second, Tebaliah the third, and Zechariah the fourth. The sons and relatives of Hosah were thirteen in all.

[12] These divisions of the gatekeepers, under their leading men, had duties for ministering in the LORD's temple, just as their relatives did. [13] They cast lots for each temple gate according to their ancestral families, young and old alike.

[14] The lot for the east gate fell to Shelemiah. They also cast lots for his son Zechariah, an insightful counselor, and his lot came out for the north gate. [15] Obed-edom's was the south gate, and his sons' lot was for the storehouses; [16] it was the west gate and the gate of Shallecheth on the ascending highway for Shuppim and Hosah.

There were guards stationed at every watch. [17] There were six Levites each day on the east, four each day on the north, four each day on the south, and two pair at the storehouses. [18] As for the court on the west, there were four at the highway and two at the court. [19] Those were the divisions of the gatekeepers from the descendants of the Korahites and Merarites.

The Levitical Treasurers and Other Officials

[20] From the Levites, Ahijah was in charge of the treasuries of God's temple and the treasuries of what had been dedicated. [21] From the sons of Ladan, who were the descendants of the Gershonites through Ladan and were the family heads belonging to Ladan the Gershonite: Jehieli. [22] The sons of Jehieli, Zetham and his brother Joel, were in charge of the treasuries of the LORD's temple.

[23] From the Amramites, the Izharites, the Hebronites, and the Uzzielites: [24] Shebuel, a descendant of Moses's son Gershom, was the officer in charge of the treasuries. [25] His relatives through Eliezer: his son Rehabiah, his son Jeshaiah, his son Joram, his son Zichri, and his son Shelomith. [26] This Shelomith and his relatives were in charge of all the treasuries of what had been dedicated by King David, by the family heads who were the commanders of thousands and of hundreds, and by the army commanders. [27] They dedicated part of the plunder from their battles for the repair of the LORD's temple. [28] All that the seer Samuel, Saul son of Kish, Abner son of Ner, and Joab son of Zeruiah had dedicated, along with everything else that had been dedicated, were in the care of Shelomith and his relatives.

[29] From the Izrahites: Chenaniah and his sons had duties outside the temple as officers and judges over Israel. [30] From the Hebronites: Hashabiah and his relatives, 1,700 capable men, had assigned duties in Israel west of the Jordan for all the work of the LORD and for the service of the king. [31] From the Hebronites: Jerijah was the head of the Hebronites, according to the family records of his ancestors. A search was made in the fortieth year of David's reign and strong, capable men were found among them at Jazer in Gilead. [32] There were among Jerijah's relatives 2,700 capable men who were family heads. King David appointed them over the Reubenites, the Gadites, and half the tribe of Manasseh as overseers in every matter relating to God and the king.

1 CHRONICLES 27

David's Secular Officials

[1] This is the list of the Israelites, the family heads, the commanders of thousands and the commanders of hundreds, and their officers who served the king in every matter to do with the divisions that were on rotated military duty each month throughout the year. There were 24,000 in each division:

[2] Jashobeam son of Zabdiel was in charge of the first division, for the first month; 24,000 were in his division. [3] He was a descendant of Perez and chief of all the army commanders for the first month.
[4] Dodai the Ahohite was in charge of the division for the second month, and Mikloth was the leader; 24,000 were in his division.
[5] The third army commander, as chief for the third month, was Benaiah son of the priest Jehoiada; 24,000 were in his division. [6] This Benaiah was a mighty man among the Thirty and over the Thirty, and his son Ammizabad was in charge of his division.
[7] The fourth commander, for the fourth month, was Joab's brother Asahel, and his son Zebadiah was commander after him; 24,000 were in his division.

8 The fifth, for the fifth month, was the commander Shamhuth the Izrahite; 24,000 were in his division.

9 The sixth, for the sixth month, was Ira son of Ikkesh the Tekoite; 24,000 were in his division.

10 The seventh, for the seventh month, was Helez the Pelonite from the descendants of Ephraim; 24,000 were in his division.

11 The eighth, for the eighth month, was Sibbecai the Hushathite, a Zerahite; 24,000 were in his division.

12 The ninth, for the ninth month, was Abiezer the Anathothite, a Benjaminite; 24,000 were in his division.

13 The tenth, for the tenth month, was Maharai the Netophathite, a Zerahite; 24,000 were in his division.

14 The eleventh, for the eleventh month, was Benaiah the Pirathonite from the descendants of Ephraim; 24,000 were in his division.

15 The twelfth, for the twelfth month, was Heldai the Netophathite, of Othniel's family; 24,000 were in his division.

16 The following were in charge of the tribes of Israel:

For the Reubenites, Eliezer son of Zichri was the chief official;

for the Simeonites, Shephatiah son of Maacah;

17 for the Levites, Hashabiah son of Kemuel; for Aaron, Zadok;

18 for Judah, Elihu, one of David's brothers; for Issachar, Omri son of Michael;

19 for Zebulun, Ishmaiah son of Obadiah;

for Naphtali, Jerimoth son of Azriel;

20 for the Ephraimites, Hoshea son of Azaziah;

for half the tribe of Manasseh, Joel son of Pedaiah;

21 for half the tribe of Manasseh in Gilead, Iddo son of Zechariah;

for Benjamin, Jaasiel son of Abner;

22 for Dan, Azarel son of Jeroham.

Those were the leaders of the tribes of Israel.

23 David didn't count the men aged twenty or under, for the Lord had said he would make Israel as numerous as the stars of the sky. 24 Joab son of Zeruiah began to count them, but he didn't complete it. There was wrath against Israel because of this census, and the number was not entered in the Historical Record of King David.

25 Azmaveth son of Adiel was in charge of the king's storehouses.

Jonathan son of Uzziah was in charge of the storehouses in the country, in the cities, in the villages, and in the fortresses.

26 Ezri son of Chelub was in charge of those who worked in the fields tilling the soil.

27 Shimei the Ramathite was in charge of the vineyards.

Zabdi the Shiphmite was in charge of the produce of the vineyards for the wine cellars.

28 Baal-hanan the Gederite was in charge of the olive and sycamore trees in the Judean foothills.

Joash was in charge of the stores of olive oil.

29 Shitrai the Sharonite was in charge of the herds that grazed in Sharon, while Shaphat son of Adlai was in charge of the herds in the valleys.

30 Obil the Ishmaelite was in charge of the camels.

Jehdeiah the Meronothite was in charge of the donkeys.

31 Jaziz the Hagrite was in charge of the flocks.

All these were officials in charge of King David's property.

32 David's uncle Jonathan was a counselor; he was a man of understanding and a scribe. Jehiel son of Hachmoni attended the king's sons. 33 Ahithophel was the king's counselor. Hushai the Archite was the king's friend. 34 After Ahithophel came Jehoiada son of Benaiah, then Abiathar. Joab was the commander of the king's army.

◗ GOING DEEPER

JOHN 10:7–10

7 Jesus said again, "Truly I tell you,

I am the gate for the sheep.

8 All who came before me are thieves and robbers, but the sheep didn't listen to them. 9 I am the gate. If anyone enters by me, he will be saved and will come in and go out and find pasture. 10 A thief comes only to steal and kill and destroy. I have come so that they may have life and have it in abundance."

David Commissions Solomon

1 CHRONICLES 28

David Commissions Solomon to Build the Temple

¹ David assembled all the leaders of Israel in Jerusalem: the leaders of the tribes, the leaders of the divisions in the king's service, the commanders of thousands and the commanders of hundreds, and the officials in charge of all the property and cattle of the king and his sons, along with the court officials, the fighting men, and all the best soldiers. ² Then King David rose to his feet and said, "Listen to me, my brothers and my people. It was in my heart to build a house as a resting place for the ark of the LORD's covenant and as a footstool for our God. I had made preparations to build, ³ but God said to me, 'You are not to build a house for my name because you are a man of war and have shed blood.'

⁴ "Yet the LORD God of Israel chose me out of all my father's family to be king over Israel forever. For he chose Judah as leader, and from the house of Judah, my father's family, and from my father's sons, he was pleased to make me king over all Israel. ⁵ And out of all my sons—for the LORD has given

me many sons—he has chosen my son Solomon to sit on the throne of the LORD's kingdom over Israel. [6] He said to me, 'Your son Solomon is the one who is to build my house and my courts, for I have chosen him to be my son, and I will be his father. [7] I will establish his kingdom forever if he perseveres in keeping my commands and my ordinances as he is doing today.'

[8] "So now in the sight of all Israel, the assembly of the LORD, and in the hearing of our God, observe and follow all the commands of the LORD your God so that you may possess this good land and leave it as an inheritance to your descendants forever.

[9] "As for you, Solomon my son, know the God of your father, and serve him wholeheartedly and with a willing mind, for the LORD searches every heart and understands the intention of every thought. If you seek him, he will be found by you, but if you abandon him, he will reject you forever. [10] Realize now that the LORD has chosen you to build a house for the sanctuary. Be strong, and do it."

[11] Then David gave his son Solomon the plans for the portico of the temple and its buildings, treasuries, upstairs rooms, inner rooms, and a room for the mercy seat. [12] The plans contained everything he had in mind for the courts of the LORD's house, all the surrounding chambers, the treasuries of God's house, and the treasuries for what is dedicated. [13] Also included were plans for the divisions of the priests and the Levites; all the work of service in the LORD's house; all the articles of service of the LORD's house; [14] the weight of gold for all the articles for every kind of service; the weight of all the silver articles for every kind of service; [15] the weight of the gold lampstands and their gold lamps, including the weight of each lampstand and its lamps; the weight of each silver lampstand and its lamps, according to

the service of each lampstand; [16] the weight of gold for each table for the rows of the Bread of the Presence and the silver for the silver tables; [17] the pure gold for the forks, sprinkling basins, and pitchers; the weight of each gold dish; the weight of each silver bowl; [18] the weight of refined gold for the altar of incense; and the plans for the chariot of the gold cherubim that spread out their wings and cover the ark of the LORD's covenant.

[19] David concluded, "By the LORD's hand on me, he enabled me to understand everything in writing, all the details of the plan."

[20] Then David said to his son Solomon, "Be strong and courageous, and do the work. Don't be afraid or discouraged, for the LORD God, my God, is with you. He won't leave you or abandon you until all the work for the service of the LORD's house is finished. [21] Here are the divisions of the priests and the Levites for all the service of God's house. Every willing person of any skill will be at your disposal for the work, and the leaders and all the people are at your every command."

1 CHRONICLES 29

Contributions for Building the Temple

[1] Then King David said to all the assembly, "My son Solomon—God has chosen him alone—is young and inexperienced. The task is great because the building will not be built for a human but for the LORD God. [2] So to the best of my ability I've made provision for the house of my God: gold for the gold articles, silver for the silver, bronze for the bronze, iron for the iron, and wood for the wood, as well as onyx, stones for mounting, antimony, stones of various colors, all kinds of precious stones, and a great quantity of marble. [3] Moreover, because of my delight in the house of my God, I now give my personal treasures of gold and silver for the house of my God over and above all that I've provided for the holy house: [4] 100 tons of gold (gold of Ophir) and 250 tons of refined silver for overlaying the walls of the buildings, [5] the gold for the gold work and the silver for the silver, for all the work to be done by the craftsmen. Now who will volunteer to consecrate himself to the LORD today?"

[6] Then the leaders of the households, the leaders of the tribes of Israel, the commanders of thousands and of hundreds, and the officials in charge of the king's work gave willingly. [7] For the service of God's house they gave 185 tons of gold and 10,000 gold coins, 375 tons of silver, 675 tons of bronze, and 4,000 tons of iron. [8] Whoever had precious stones gave them to the treasury of the LORD's house under the care of Jehiel the Gershonite. [9] Then the people rejoiced because of their leaders' willingness to give, for they had given to the LORD wholeheartedly. King David also rejoiced greatly.

David's Prayer

[10] Then David blessed the LORD in the sight of all the assembly. David said,

May you be blessed, LORD God of our father Israel, from eternity to eternity. [11] Yours, LORD, is the greatness and the power and the glory and the splendor and the majesty, for everything in the heavens and on earth belongs to you. Yours, LORD, is the kingdom, and you are exalted as head over all. [12] Riches and honor come from you, and you are the ruler of everything. Power and might are in your hand, and it is in your hand to make great and to give strength to all. [13] Now therefore, our God, we give you thanks and praise your glorious name.

[14] But who am I, and who are my people, that we should be able to give as generously as this? For everything comes from you, and we have given you only what comes from your own hand. [15] For we are aliens and temporary residents in your presence as were all our ancestors. Our days on earth are like a shadow, without hope. [16] LORD our God, all this wealth that we've provided for building you a house for your holy name comes from your hand; everything belongs to you. [17] I know, my God, that you test the heart and that you are pleased with what is right. I have willingly given all these things with an upright heart, and now I have seen your people who are present here giving joyfully and willingly to you. [18] LORD God of Abraham, Isaac, and Israel, our ancestors, keep this desire forever in the thoughts of the hearts of your people, and confirm their hearts toward you. [19] Give my son Solomon an undivided heart to keep and to carry out all your

commands, your decrees, and your statutes, and to build the building for which I have made provision.

[20] Then David said to the whole assembly, "Blessed be the LORD your God." So the whole assembly praised the LORD God of their ancestors. They knelt low and paid homage to the LORD and the king.

[21] The following day they offered sacrifices to the LORD and burnt offerings to the LORD: a thousand bulls, a thousand rams, and a thousand lambs, along with their drink offerings, and sacrifices in abundance for all Israel. [22] They ate and drank with great joy in the LORD's presence that day.

The Enthronement of Solomon

Then, for a second time, they made David's son Solomon king; they anointed him as the LORD's ruler, and Zadok as the priest. [23] Solomon sat on the LORD's throne as king in place of his father David. He prospered, and all Israel obeyed him. [24] All the leaders and the mighty men, and all of King David's sons as well, pledged their allegiance to King Solomon. [25] The LORD highly exalted Solomon in the sight of all Israel and bestowed on him such royal majesty as had not been bestowed on any king over Israel before him.

A Summary of David's Life

[26] David son of Jesse was king over all Israel. [27] The length of his reign over Israel was forty years; he reigned in Hebron for seven years and in Jerusalem for thirty-three. [28] He died at a good old age, full of days, riches, and honor, and his son Solomon became king in his place. [29] As for the events of King David's reign, from beginning to end, note that they are written in the Events of the Seer Samuel, the Events of the Prophet Nathan, and the Events of the Seer Gad, [30] along with all his reign, his might, and the incidents that affected him and Israel and all the kingdoms of the surrounding lands.

◗ GOING DEEPER

PSALM 132:11–12

[11] The LORD swore an oath to David,
a promise he will not abandon:

"I will set one of your offspring
on your throne.

[12] If your sons keep my covenant
and my decrees that I will teach them,
their sons will also sit on your throne forever."

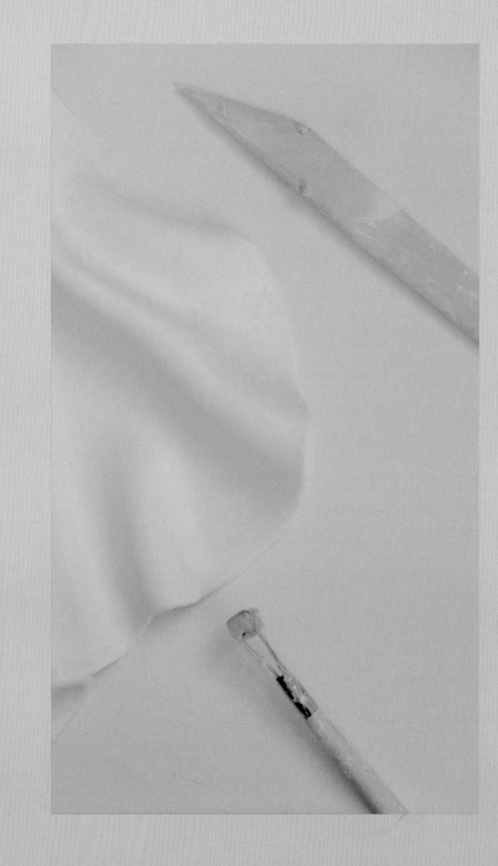

DAY 19

WEEK 3

Solomon's Request for Wisdom

2 CHRONICLES 1

Solomon's Request for Wisdom

[1] Solomon son of David strengthened his hold on his kingdom. The LORD his God was with him and highly exalted him. [2] Then Solomon spoke to all Israel, to the commanders of thousands and of hundreds, to the judges, and to every leader in all Israel—the family heads. [3] Solomon and the whole assembly with him went to the high place that was in Gibeon because God's tent of meeting, which the LORD's servant Moses had made in the wilderness, was there. [4] Now David had brought the ark of God from Kiriath-jearim to the place he had set up for it, because he had pitched a tent for it in Jerusalem, [5] but he put the bronze altar, which Bezalel son of Uri, son of Hur, had made, in front of the LORD's tabernacle. Solomon and the assembly inquired of him there. [6] Solomon offered sacrifices there in the LORD's presence on the bronze altar at the tent of meeting; he offered a thousand burnt offerings on it.

[7] That night God appeared to Solomon and said to him, "Ask. What should I give you?"

[8] And Solomon said to God, "You have shown great and faithful love to my father David, and you have made me king in his place. [9] LORD God, let your promise to my father David now come true. For you have made me king over a people as numerous as the dust of the earth. [10] Now grant me wisdom and knowledge so that I may lead these people, for who can judge this great people of yours?"

[11] God said to Solomon, "Since this was in your heart, and you have not requested riches, wealth, or glory, or for the life of those who hate you, and you have not even requested long life, but you have requested for yourself wisdom and knowledge that you may judge my people over whom I have made you king, [12] wisdom and knowledge are given to you. I will also give you riches, wealth, and glory, unlike what was given to the kings who were before you, or will be given to those after you." [13] So Solomon went to Jerusalem from the high place that was in Gibeon in front of the tent of meeting, and he reigned over Israel.

Solomon's Horses and Wealth

[14] Solomon accumulated 1,400 chariots and 12,000 horsemen, which he stationed in the chariot cities and with the king in Jerusalem. [15] The king made silver and gold as common in Jerusalem as stones, and he made cedar as abundant as sycamore in the Judean foothills. [16] Solomon's horses came from Egypt and Kue. The king's traders would get them from Kue at the going price. [17] A chariot could be imported from Egypt for fifteen pounds of silver and a horse for nearly four pounds. In the same way, they exported them to all the kings of the Hittites and to the kings of Aram through their agents.

2 CHRONICLES 2

Solomon's Letter to Hiram

[1] Solomon decided to build a temple for the name of the LORD and a royal palace for himself, [2] so he assigned 70,000 men as porters, 80,000 men as stonecutters in the mountains, and 3,600 as supervisors over them.

[3] Then Solomon sent word to King Hiram of Tyre:

Do for me what you did for my father David. You sent him cedars to build him a house to live in. [4] Now I am building a temple for the name of the LORD my God in order to dedicate it to him for burning fragrant incense before him, for displaying the rows of the Bread of the Presence continuously, and for sacrificing burnt offerings for the morning and the evening, the Sabbaths and the New Moons, and the appointed festivals of the LORD our God. This is ordained for Israel permanently. [5] The temple that I am building will be great, for our God is greater than any of the gods. [6] But who is able to build a temple for him, since even heaven and the highest heaven cannot contain him? Who am I then that I should build a temple for him except as a place to burn incense before him? [7] Therefore, send me an artisan who is skilled in engraving to work with gold, silver, bronze, and iron, and with purple, crimson, and blue yarn. He will work with the artisans who are with me in Judah and Jerusalem, appointed by my father David. [8] Also, send me cedar, cypress, and algum logs from Lebanon, for I know that your servants know how to cut the trees of Lebanon. Note that my servants will be with your servants [9] to prepare logs for me in abundance because the temple I am building will be great and wondrous. [10] I will give your servants, the woodcutters who cut the trees, one hundred twenty thousand bushels of wheat flour, one hundred twenty thousand bushels of barley, one hundred twenty thousand gallons of wine, and one hundred twenty thousand gallons of oil.

Hiram's Reply

[11] Then King Hiram of Tyre wrote a letter and sent it to Solomon:

Because the LORD loves his people, he set you over them as king.

[12] Hiram also said:

Blessed be the LORD God of Israel, who made the heavens and the earth! He gave King David a wise son with insight and understanding, who will build a temple for the LORD and a royal palace for himself. [13] I have now sent Huram-abi, a skillful man who has understanding. [14] He is the son of a woman from the daughters of Dan. His father is a man of Tyre. He knows how to work with gold, silver, bronze, iron, stone, and wood, with purple, blue, crimson yarn, and fine linen. He knows how to do all kinds of engraving and to execute any design that may be given him. I have sent him to be with your artisans and the artisans of my lord, your father David. [15] Now, let my lord send the wheat, barley, oil, and wine to his servants as promised. [16] We will cut logs from Lebanon, as many as you need, and bring them to you as rafts by sea to Joppa. You can then take them up to Jerusalem.

Solomon's Workforce

NOTES

[17] Solomon took a census of all the resident alien men in the land of Israel, after the census that his father David had conducted, and the total was 153,600.
[18] Solomon made 70,000 of them porters, 80,000 stonecutters in the mountains, and 3,600 supervisors to make the people work.

GOING DEEPER

JOHN 15:4–7

[4] "Remain in me, and I in you. Just as a branch is unable to produce fruit by itself unless it remains on the vine, neither can you unless you remain in me. [5] I am the
vine; you are the branches. The one who remains in me and I in him produces much fruit, because you can do nothing without me. [6] If anyone does not remain
in me, he is thrown aside like a branch and he withers. They gather them, throw them into the fire, and they are burned.

[7] If you remain in me and my words remain in you, ask whatever you want and it will be done for you."

Chocolate Pomegranate Drops

Prep Time	Cook Time	Yields
10 MINUTES	**3 MINUTES**	**15–20 DROPS**

INGREDIENTS

2 pomegranates

1 (12-ounce) bag
semi-sweet
chocolate chips

— Remove seeds from the pomegranates or buy them pre-removed. If you're removing the seeds (which resemble grains of corn), use a sharp knife to score the outside skin of the pomegranate.

— Fill a medium-sized mixing bowl with water and break the pomegranate open under the water. This prevents the juice from spraying and the seeds will sink to the bottom, separating from the pulp, which will float to the top. Rinse and strain the seeds. Dry the outside of the seeds completely.

— Melt chocolate chips either on the stove or in a microwave-safe dish. If you're using the microwave, heat half of the bag at a time and stir frequently until completely melted.

— Set aside a small portion of seeds for garnishing. Gently mix remaining seeds with the melted chocolate. Some people prefer more chocolate or more pomegranates, so you can play with the proportions.

— Spoon tablespoonfuls of the chocolate-pomegranate mixture onto a baking sheet that has been covered in wax or parchment paper. Garnish each clump with a few non-chocolatey pomegranate seeds for presentation. Chill in the refrigerator 30 to 45 minutes until they harden.

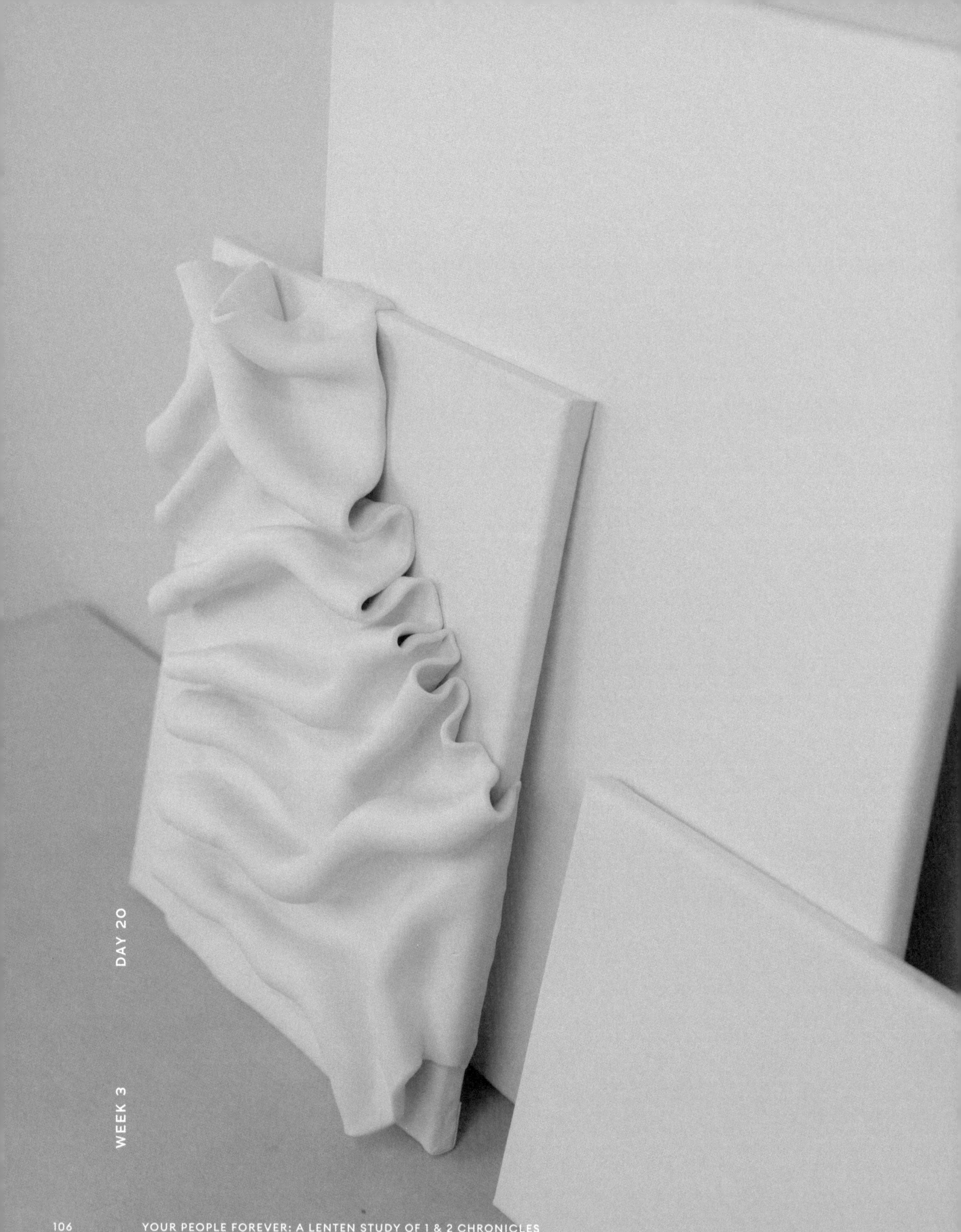

WEEK 3 DAY 20

Grace Day

Therefore, brothers and sisters, in view of the mercies of God, I urge you to present your bodies as a living sacrifice, holy and pleasing to God; this is your true worship.

ROMANS 12:1

Take this day to catch up on your reading, pray, and rest in the presence of the Lord.

Weekly Truth

Scripture is God-breathed and true. When we memorize it, we carry His Word with us wherever we go.

We are continuing to memorize 1 Chronicles 29:11–13. Let's add verse 12, thanking God for the strength and provision that only comes from Him.

See tips for memorizing Scripture on page 240.

Yours, LORD, is the greatness and the power and the glory and the splendor and the majesty, for everything in the heavens and on earth belongs to you. Yours, LORD, is the kingdom, and you are exalted as head over all. Riches and honor come from you, and you are the ruler of everything. Power and might are in your hand, and it is in your hand to make great and to give strength to all. Now therefore, our God, we give you thanks and praise your glorious name.

1 CHRONICLES 29:11–13

Building the Temple

2 CHRONICLES 3

Building the Temple

¹ Then Solomon began to build the LORD's temple in Jerusalem on Mount Moriah where the LORD had appeared to his father David,

at the site David had prepared on the threshing floor of Ornan the Jebusite. ² He began to build on the second day of the second month in the fourth year of his reign. ³ These are Solomon's foundations for building God's temple: the length was ninety feet, and the width thirty feet. ⁴ The portico, which was across the front extending across the width of the temple, was thirty feet wide; its height was thirty feet; he overlaid its inner surface with pure gold. ⁵ The larger room he paneled with cypress wood, overlaid with fine gold, and decorated with palm trees and chains. ⁶ He adorned the temple with precious stones for beauty, and the gold was the gold of Parvaim. ⁷ He overlaid the temple—the beams, the thresholds, its walls and doors—with gold, and he carved cherubim on the walls.

The Most Holy Place

[8] Then he made the most holy place; its length corresponded to the width of the temple, [30] feet, and its width was 30 feet. He overlaid it with forty-five thousand pounds of fine gold. [9] The weight of the nails was twenty ounces of gold, and he overlaid the ceiling with gold.

[10] He made two cherubim of sculptured work, for the most holy place, and he overlaid them with gold. [11] The overall length of the wings of the cherubim was 30 feet: the wing of one was 7½ feet, touching the wall of the room; its other wing was 7½ feet, touching the wing of the other cherub. [12] The wing of the other cherub was 7½ feet, touching the wall of the room; its other wing was 7½ feet, reaching the wing of the other cherub. [13] The wingspan of these cherubim was 30 feet. They stood on their feet and faced the larger room.

[14] He made the curtain of blue, purple, and crimson yarn and fine linen, and he wove cherubim into it.

The Bronze Pillars

[15] In front of the temple he made two pillars, each 27 feet high. The capital on top of each was 7½ feet high. [16] He had made chainwork in the inner sanctuary and also put it on top of the pillars. He made a hundred pomegranates and fastened them into the chainwork. [17] Then he set up the pillars in front of the sanctuary, one on the right and one on the left. He named the one on the right Jachin and the one on the left Boaz.

2 CHRONICLES 4

The Altar and Basins

[1] He made a bronze altar 30 feet long, 30 feet wide, and 15 feet high.

[2] Then he made the cast metal basin, 15 feet from brim to brim, perfectly round. It was 7½ feet high and 45 feet in circumference. [3] The likeness of oxen was below it, completely encircling it, ten every half yard, completely surrounding the basin. The oxen were cast in two rows when the basin was cast. [4] It stood on twelve oxen, three facing north, three facing west, three facing south, and three facing east. The basin was on top of them and all their hindquarters were toward the center. [5] The basin was three inches thick, and its rim was fashioned like the brim of a cup or a lily blossom. It could hold eleven thousand gallons.

[6] He made ten basins for washing and he put five on the right and five on the left. The parts of the burnt offering were rinsed in them, but the basin was used by the priests for washing.

The Lampstands, Tables, and Courts

[7] He made the ten gold lampstands according to their specifications and put them in the sanctuary, five on the right and five on the left. [8] He made ten tables and placed them in the sanctuary, five on the right and five on the left. He also made a hundred gold bowls.

[9] He made the courtyard of the priests and the large court, and doors for the court. He overlaid the doors with bronze. [10] He put the basin on the right side, toward the southeast. [11] Then Huram made the pots, the shovels, and the bowls.

Completion of the Bronze Furnishings

So Huram finished doing the work that he was doing for King Solomon in God's temple: [12] two pillars; the bowls and the capitals on top of the two pillars; the two gratings for covering both bowls of the capitals that were on top of the pillars; [13] the four hundred pomegranates for the two gratings (two rows of pomegranates for each grating covering both capitals' bowls on top of the pillars). [14] He also made the water carts and the basins on the water carts. [15] The one basin and the twelve oxen underneath it, [16] the pots, the shovels, the forks, and all their utensils—Huram-abi made them for King Solomon for the LORD's temple. All these were made of polished bronze. [17] The king had them cast in clay molds in the Jordan Valley between Succoth and Zeredah. [18] Solomon made all these utensils in such great abundance that the weight of the bronze was not determined.

NOTES

Completion of the Gold Furnishings

[19] Solomon also made all the equipment in God's temple: the gold altar; the tables on which to put the Bread of the Presence; [20] the lampstands and their lamps of pure gold to burn in front of the inner sanctuary according to specifications; [21] the flowers, lamps, and gold tongs—of purest gold; [22] the wick trimmers, sprinkling basins, ladles, and firepans—of purest gold; and the entryway to the temple, its inner doors to the most holy place, and the doors of the temple sanctuary—of gold.

2 CHRONICLES 5

[1] So all the work Solomon did for the Lord's temple was completed. Then Solomon brought the consecrated things of his father David—the silver, the gold, and all the utensils—and put them in the treasuries of God's temple.

Preparations for the Temple Dedication

[2] At that time Solomon assembled at Jerusalem the elders of Israel—all the tribal heads, the ancestral chiefs of the Israelites—in order to bring the ark of the covenant of the Lord up from the city of David, that is, Zion. [3] So all the men of Israel were assembled in the king's presence at the festival; this was in the seventh month.

[4] All the elders of Israel came, and the Levites picked up the ark. [5] They brought up the ark, the tent of meeting, and the holy utensils that were in the tent. The priests and the Levites brought them up. [6] King Solomon and the entire congregation of Israel who had gathered around him were in front of the ark sacrificing sheep, goats, and cattle that could not be counted or numbered because there were so many. [7] The priests brought the ark of the Lord's covenant to its place, into the inner sanctuary of the temple, to the most holy place, beneath the wings of the cherubim. [8] And the cherubim spread their wings over the place of the ark so that the cherubim formed a cover above the ark and its poles. [9] The poles were so long that their ends were seen from the holy place in front of the inner sanctuary, but they were not seen from outside; they are still there today. [10] Nothing was in the ark except the two tablets that Moses had put in it at Horeb, where the Lord had made a covenant with the Israelites when they came out of Egypt.

[11] Now all the priests who were present had consecrated themselves regardless of their divisions. When the priests came out of the holy place, [12] the Levitical singers dressed in fine linen and carrying cymbals, harps,

and lyres were standing east of the altar, and with them were 120 priests blowing trumpets. The Levitical singers were descendants of Asaph, Heman, and Jeduthun and their sons and relatives. [13] The trumpeters and singers joined together to praise and thank the LORD with one voice. They raised their voices, accompanied by trumpets, cymbals, and musical instruments, in praise to the LORD:

> For he is good;
> his faithful love endures forever.

The temple, the LORD's temple, was filled with a cloud.

[14] And because of the cloud, the priests were not able to continue ministering, for the glory of the LORD filled God's temple.

◗ GOING DEEPER

EXODUS 26:31-35

[31] "You are to make a curtain of blue, purple, and scarlet yarn, and finely spun linen with a design of cherubim worked into it. [32] Hang it on four gold-plated pillars of acacia wood that have gold hooks and that stand on four silver bases. [33] Hang the curtain under the clasps and bring the ark of the testimony there behind the curtain, so the curtain will make a separation for you between the holy place and the most holy place. [34] Put the mercy seat on the ark of the testimony in the most holy place. [35] Place the table outside the curtain and the lampstand on the south side of the tabernacle, opposite the table; put the table on the north side."

HEBREWS 9:11-14

New Covenant Ministry

[11] But Christ has appeared as a high priest of the good things that have come. In the greater and more perfect tabernacle not made with hands (that is, not of this creation), [12] he entered the most holy place once for all time, not by the blood of goats and calves, but by his own blood, having obtained eternal redemption. [13] For if the blood of goats and bulls and the ashes of a young cow, sprinkling those who are defiled, sanctify for the purification of the flesh, [14] how much more will the blood of Christ, who through the eternal Spirit offered himself without blemish to God, cleanse our consciences from dead works so that we can serve the living God?

Solomon's Temple

Solomon started building the temple on Mount Moriah in Jerusalem in 967 BC and completed it seven years later (2Ch 3:1-2; 5:1; 1Kg 6:1, 38). Symbolizing God's presence and rule over all creation, the temple was a place of worship where God could dwell with His people. Each aspect of the temple structure prepared the worshiper to repent, remember God's promises and faithfulness, and both physically and spiritually draw nearer to the presence of God.

OPEN HERE

fellowship offerings (1Kg 9:25),
et high by 30 feet long
st prominent object in the
as kept burning on the altar
he altar is where the priests
ipers brought as confession
ommunicated the worshiper's
o be restored to God, and
re of God's grace and mercy in
a substitute for the individual

—22

d *Jachin*, "He Will Establish."
Boaz, "In Him Is Strength."
d the rule of God and the
y have also represented the
garden of Eden.

wide by 30 feet deep and
o the Holy Place.

d Wooden Doors
5

arated the Holy Place from the
ld enter through these doors.

8 / The Holy Place
2CH 3:5–7; 4:7–8; 1KG 6:15, 17–18, 29–30; 7:48–49

The Holy Place contained the golden altar of incense, the golden table for the Bread of the Presence, ten golden lampstands, and other furnishings. The ceilings were fir or cypress, overlaid with gold and engraved with images of cherubim, palm trees, and open flowers. It measured 60 feet long by 30 feet wide. In this smaller space, the priests carried out many of their daily duties to care for the temple. The priests were representatives of the people before God.

9 / The Lampstands
1KG 7:49; EX 25:31–32

The tabernacle lampstand consisted of a gold base and shaft with six branches going out on the sides and floral details. The lampstand was constantly lit, and it served as a reminder of God's active presence among His people. The ten lampstands described in Chronicles may have included this lampstand, or have been additional pieces in Solomon's temple.

10 / Inner Gold-Covered Wooden Doors
2CH 4:22; 1KG 6:31–32

These ornate doors separated the Most Holy Place from the Holy Place. Only the high priest could enter these doors once a year.

11 / The Most Holy Place (or the Holy of Holies)
2CH 3:8–14; 1KG 6:15–16, 18–20, 22–30

The inner sanctuary was 30 feet long by 30 feet wide. It contained two large golden cherubim, which stood on either side of the ark of the covenant with wings stretched from wall to wall and meeting in the center over the ark. Each cherub was 15 feet tall with a 15-foot wingspan. This space was where God dwelt with His people. Only the high priest could enter once a year on the Day of Atonement, when he would lay his hands on the head of a male goat and confess over it all of his own sins and the sins of the people before God.

The Courtyard
2CH 4:9; 1KG 6:36; 1KG 7:9

The temple was enclosed in an outer and inner courtyard. Nearly any worshiper could enter the courtyard to bring a sacrifice. They would enter through the front entry and move forward toward the rear sanctuary, moving from a large, public space toward the smaller, intimate inner temple where only priests could enter. Many of the elements in the courtyard reflected elements of creation and the garden of Eden.

Large Metal Basin (Called "The Sea")
2CH 4:2–6; 1KG 7:23–26

Supported by twelve bronze oxen arranged in sets of three, the basin measured 7½ feet high, 15 feet in diameter, and held 11,000 gallons of water. The basin was used for the priests' ceremonial washing (2Ch 4:6). In the ancient Near East, the sea represented chaos. Some scholars suggest that the basin served as a reminder of the creation story in Genesis, where God brought order from chaos and demonstrated His power over all creation.

Ten Basins
2CH 4:6; 1KG 7:27–40

The ten basins were on bronze frames with bronze wheels. They were decorated with carved cherubim, lions, palm trees, and wreaths. These basins contained water for the priests to wash animal parts before using them in burnt offerings.

Bronze Altar
2CH 4:1

Used for both burnt and
the altar measured 15 fe
and wide. It was the mo
courtyard, and the fire v
continuously (Lv 6:13). T
offered sacrifices worsh
of sin. These offerings c
awareness of the need
presented a public pictu
offering forgiveness and
(Lv 1–2; 4–7).

Bronze Pillars
2CH 3:15–17; 1KG 7:15

The right pillar was calle
The left pillar was called
These pillars represente
Davidic dynasty, and ma
tree of life found in the

Portico
2CH 3:4; 1KG 6:3

The portico was 30 feet
served as the entrance

Outer Gold-Covere
2CH 4:22; 1KG 6:33–3

These ornate doors sepa
portico. Only priests cou

The Dedication of the Temple

2 CHRONICLES 6

Solomon's Dedication of the Temple

[1] Then Solomon said:

The LORD said he would dwell in total darkness,
[2] but I have built an exalted temple for you,
a place for your dwelling forever.

[3] Then the king turned and blessed the entire congregation of Israel while they were standing. [4] He said:

Blessed be the LORD God of Israel!
He spoke directly to my father David,
and he has fulfilled the promise
by his power.
He said,
[5] "Since the day I brought my people Israel
out of the land of Egypt,
I have not chosen a city to build a temple in
among any of the tribes of Israel,
so that my name would be there,
and I have not chosen a man
to be ruler over my people Israel.
[6] But I have chosen Jerusalem
so that my name will be there,
and I have chosen David
to be over my people Israel."
[7] My father David had his heart set
on building a temple for the name of the LORD, the God
of Israel.
[8] However, the LORD said to my father David,
"Since it was your desire to build a temple for my name,
you have done well to have this desire.

[9] Yet, you are not the one to build the temple,
but your son, your own offspring,
will build the temple for my name."
[10] So the LORD has fulfilled what he promised.
I have taken the place of my father David
and I sit on the throne of Israel, as the LORD promised.
I have built the temple for the name of the LORD,
the God of Israel.
[11] I have put the ark there,
where the LORD's covenant is
that he made with the Israelites.

Solomon's Prayer

[12] Then Solomon stood before the altar of the LORD in front of the entire congregation of Israel and spread out his hands. [13] For Solomon had made a bronze platform 7½ feet long, 7½ feet wide, and 4½ feet high and put it in the court. He stood on it, knelt down in front of the entire congregation of Israel, and spread out his hands toward heaven. [14] He said:

LORD God of Israel,
there is no God like you
in heaven or on earth,
who keeps his gracious covenant
with your servants who walk before you
with all their heart.
[15] You have kept what you promised
to your servant, my father David.
You spoke directly to him,
and you fulfilled your promise by your power,
as it is today.

16 Therefore, LORD God of Israel,
keep what you promised
to your servant, my father David:
"You will never fail to have a man
to sit before me on the throne of Israel,
if only your sons take care to walk in my Law
as you have walked before me."
17 Now, LORD God of Israel, please confirm
what you promised to your servant David.
18 But will God indeed live on earth with humans?
Even heaven, the highest heaven, cannot contain you,
much less this temple I have built.
19 Listen to your servant's prayer and his petition,
LORD my God,
so that you may hear the cry and the prayer
that your servant prays before you,
20 so that your eyes watch over this temple
day and night,
toward the place where you said
you would put your name;
and so that you may hear the prayer
your servant prays toward this place.
21 Hear the petitions of your servant
and your people Israel,
which they pray toward this place.
May you hear in your dwelling place in heaven.
May you hear and forgive.
22 If a man sins against his neighbor
and is forced to take an oath
and he comes to take an oath
before your altar in this temple,
23 may you hear in heaven and act.
May you judge your servants,
condemning the wicked man by bringing
what he has done on his own head
and providing justice for the righteous
by rewarding him according to his righteousness.
24 If your people Israel are defeated before an enemy,
because they have sinned against you,
and they return to you and praise your name,
and they pray and plead for mercy
before you in this temple,
25 may you hear in heaven

and forgive the sin of your people Israel.
May you restore them to the land
you gave them and their ancestors.
26 When the skies are shut and there is no rain
because they have sinned against you,
and they pray toward this place
and praise your name,
and they turn from their sins
because you are afflicting them,
27 may you hear in heaven
and forgive the sin of your servants
and your people Israel,
so that you may teach them the good way
they should walk in.
May you send rain on your land
that you gave your people for an inheritance.
28 When there is famine in the land,
when there is pestilence,
when there is blight or mildew, locust or grasshopper,
when their enemies besiege them
in the land and its cities,
when there is any plague or illness,
29 every prayer or petition
that any person or that all your people Israel may have—
they each know their own affliction and suffering—
as they spread out their hands toward this temple,
30 may you hear in heaven, your dwelling place,
and may you forgive and give to everyone
according to all their ways, since you know each heart,
for you alone know the human heart,
31 so that they may fear you
and walk in your ways
all the days they live on the land
you gave our ancestors.
32 Even for the foreigner who is not of your people Israel
but has come from a distant land
because of your great name
and your strong hand and outstretched arm:
when he comes and prays toward this temple,
33 may you hear in heaven in your dwelling place,
and do all the foreigner asks you.
Then all the peoples of the earth will know your name,
to fear you as your people Israel do

and know that this temple I have built

bears your name.

[34] When your people go out to fight against their enemies,

wherever you send them,

and they pray to you

in the direction of this city you have chosen

and the temple that I have built for your name,

[35] may you hear their prayer and petition in heaven

and uphold their cause.

[36] When they sin against you—

for there is no one who does not sin—

and you are angry with them

and hand them over to the enemy,

and their captors deport them

to a distant or nearby country,

[37] and when they come to their senses

in the land where they were deported

and repent and petition you in their captors' land,

saying, "We have sinned and done wrong;

we have been wicked,"

[38] and when they return to you with all their mind and all their heart

in the land of their captivity where they were taken captive,

and when they pray in the direction of their land

that you gave their ancestors,

and the city you have chosen,

and toward the temple I have built for your name,

[39] may you hear their prayer and petitions in heaven,

your dwelling place,

and uphold their cause.

May you forgive your people

who sinned against you.

[40] Now, my God,

please let your eyes be open

and your ears attentive

to the prayer of this place.

[41] Now therefore:

Arise, Lord God, come to your resting place,

you and your powerful ark.

May your priests, Lord God, be clothed with salvation,

and may your faithful people rejoice in goodness.

[42] Lord God, do not reject your anointed one;

remember your servant David's acts of faithful love.

2 CHRONICLES 7

The Dedication Ceremonies

¹ When Solomon finished praying, fire descended from heaven and consumed the burnt offering and the sacrifices, and the glory of the LORD filled the temple. ² The priests were not able to enter the LORD's temple because the glory of the LORD filled the temple of the LORD. ³ All the Israelites were watching when the fire descended and the glory of the LORD came on the temple. They bowed down on the pavement with their faces to the ground. They worshiped and praised the LORD:

> For he is good,
> for his faithful love endures forever.

⁴ The king and all the people were offering sacrifices in the LORD's presence. ⁵ King Solomon offered a sacrifice of twenty-two thousand cattle and one hundred twenty thousand sheep and goats. In this manner the king and all the people dedicated God's temple. ⁶ The priests and the Levites were standing at their stations. The Levites had the musical instruments of the LORD, which King David had made to give thanks to the LORD—"for his faithful love endures forever"—when he offered praise with them. Across from the Levites, the priests were blowing trumpets, and all the people were standing. ⁷ Since the bronze altar that Solomon had made could not accommodate the burnt offering, the grain offering, and the fat of the fellowship offerings, Solomon first consecrated the middle of the courtyard that was in front of the LORD's temple and then offered the burnt offerings and the fat of the fellowship offerings there.

⁸ So Solomon and all Israel with him—a very great assembly, from the entrance to Hamath to the Brook of Egypt—observed the festival at that time for seven days. ⁹ On the eighth day they held a solemn assembly, for the dedication of the altar lasted seven days and the festival seven days. ¹⁰ On the twenty-third day of the seventh month he sent the people home, rejoicing and with happy hearts for the goodness the LORD had done for David, for Solomon, and for his people Israel.

¹¹ So Solomon finished the LORD's temple and the royal palace. Everything that had entered Solomon's heart to do for the LORD's temple and for his own palace succeeded.

The LORD's Response

¹² Then the LORD appeared to Solomon at night and said to him:

I have heard your prayer and have chosen this place for myself as a temple of sacrifice. ¹³ If I shut the sky so there is no rain, or if I command the grasshopper to consume the land, or if I send pestilence on my people, ¹⁴ and my people, who bear my name, humble themselves, pray and seek my face, and turn from their evil ways, then I will hear from heaven, forgive their sin, and heal their land. [15] My eyes will now be open and my ears attentive to prayer from this place. [16] And I have now chosen and consecrated this temple so that my name may be there forever; my eyes and my heart will be there at all times.

[17] As for you, if you walk before me as your father David walked, doing everything I have commanded you, and if you keep my statutes and ordinances, [18] I will establish your royal throne, as I promised your father David: You will never fail to have a man ruling in Israel.

[19] However, if you turn away and abandon my statutes and my commands that I have set before you and if you go and serve other gods and bow in worship to them, [20] then I will uproot Israel from the soil that I gave them, and this temple that I have sanctified for my name I will banish from my presence; I will make it an object of scorn and ridicule among all the peoples. [21] As for this temple, which was exalted, everyone who passes by will be appalled and will say, "Why did the LORD do this to this land and this temple?" [22] Then they will say, "Because they abandoned the LORD God of their ancestors who brought them out of the land of Egypt. They clung to other gods and bowed in worship to them and served them. Because of this, he brought all this ruin on them."

🔖 GOING DEEPER

JOHN 1:14

The Word became flesh and dwelt among us. We observed his glory, the glory as the one and only Son from the Father, full of grace and truth.

Repent

Here at the center of the Lenten season, pause and consider God's invitation for repentance— to turn away from sin and back toward God.

As Chronicles reminds us, God's people were identified by two realities: covenant relationship with Him, and proper worship that was an overflow of this relationship. In 2 Chronicles 6 and 7, we read a pivotal moment in Israel's history—the dedication of the temple and God's response to its completion. At the temple's dedication, Solomon prays on behalf of the congregation of Israel, asking God to be present and receptive to His people's prayers (2Ch 6:12–42). In response, God promises His presence, keeping His eyes open and His ears attentive to the prayers offered in the temple (2Ch 7:12–16).

Like Chronicles, Lent is an invitation to reorient our lives toward right relationship with and right worship of the one true God. While a temple is no longer needed for God to accept us because of Christ's sacrifice, resurrection, and ascension (Heb 9:11–14), we still need to humble ourselves in prayer, turning from sin and toward God's presence (2Ch 7:14).

"Repentance" is the act of turning to God with sincere remorse over the ways we've deviated from what God intended. Use this space to write a prayer of repentance to God. Let the words of 2 Chronicles 7:14–15 remind you that He sees and hears you.

Lord God, of my heart, my life, my world— Reveal what I truly need to say to you. Where have I turned away?

- discontentment (this life chapter)

- discouragement

- undervaluing (grief/trauma) (self)

- chasing after relief

- harshness (to self)

These are not where you intend me to live. I'm sorry I left your Good will. Forgive me & heal me, I want to go on with you.

"...and my people, who bear my name, humble themselves, pray and seek my face, and turn from their evil ways, then I will hear from heaven, forgive their sin, and heal their land. My eyes will now be open and my ears attentive to prayer from this place."

2 CHRONICLES 7:14–15

The Queen of Sheba Seeks Solomon's Wisdom

2 CHRONICLES 8

Solomon's Later Building Projects

¹ At the end of twenty years during which Solomon had built the LORD's temple and his own palace— ² Solomon had rebuilt the cities Hiram gave him and settled Israelites there— ³ Solomon went to Hamath-zobah and seized it. ⁴ He built Tadmor in the wilderness along with all the storage cities that he built in Hamath. ⁵ He built Upper Beth-horon and Lower Beth-horon—fortified cities with walls, gates, and bars— ⁶ Baalath, all the storage cities that belonged to Solomon, all the chariot cities, the cavalry cities, and everything Solomon desired to build in Jerusalem, Lebanon, or anywhere else in the land of his dominion.

⁷ As for all the peoples who remained of the Hethites, Amorites, Perizzites, Hivites, and Jebusites, who were not from Israel— ⁸ their descendants who remained in the land after them, those the Israelites had not completely destroyed—Solomon imposed forced labor on them; it is

this way today. [9] But Solomon did not consign the Israelites to be slaves for his work; they were soldiers, commanders of his captains, and commanders of his chariots and his cavalry. [10] These were King Solomon's deputies: 250 who supervised the people.

[11] Solomon brought the daughter of Pharaoh from the city of David to the house he had built for her, for he said, "My wife must not live in the house of King David of Israel because the places the ark of the LORD has come into are holy."

Public Worship Established at the Temple

[12] At that time Solomon offered burnt offerings to the LORD on the LORD's altar he had made in front of the portico. [13] He followed the daily requirement for offerings according to the commandment of Moses for Sabbaths, New Moons, and the three annual appointed festivals: the Festival of Unleavened Bread, the Festival of Weeks, and the Festival of Shelters. [14] According to the ordinances of his father David,

he appointed the divisions of the priests over their service, of the Levites over their responsibilities to offer praise and to minister before the priests following the daily requirement, and of the gatekeepers by their divisions with respect to each temple gate, for this had been the command of David, the man of God. [15] They did not turn aside from the king's command regarding the priests and the Levites concerning any matter or concerning the treasuries. [16] All of Solomon's work was carried out from the day the foundation was laid for the LORD's temple until it was finished. So the LORD's temple was completed.

Solomon's Fleet

[17] At that time Solomon went to Ezion-geber and to Eloth on the seashore in the land of Edom. [18] So Hiram sent ships to him by his servants along with crews of experienced seamen. They went with Solomon's servants to Ophir, took from there seventeen tons of gold, and delivered it to King Solomon.

2 CHRONICLES 9

The Queen of Sheba

¹ The queen of Sheba heard of Solomon's fame, so she came to test Solomon with difficult questions at Jerusalem with a very large entourage, with camels bearing spices, gold in abundance, and precious stones. She came to Solomon and spoke with him about everything that was on her mind. ² So Solomon answered all her questions; nothing was too difficult for Solomon to explain to her. ³ When the queen of Sheba observed Solomon's wisdom, the palace he had built, ⁴ the food at his table, his servants' residence, his attendants' service and their attire, his cupbearers and their attire, and the burnt offerings he offered at the LORD's temple, it took her breath away.

⁵ She said to the king, "The report I heard in my own country about your words and about your wisdom is true. ⁶ But I didn't believe their reports until I came and saw with my own eyes. Indeed, I was not even told half of your great wisdom! You far exceed the report I heard. ⁷ How happy are your men. How happy are these servants of yours, who always stand in your presence hearing your wisdom. ⁸ Blessed be the LORD your God! He delighted in you and put you on his throne as king for the LORD your God. Because your God loved Israel enough to establish them forever, he has set you over them as king to carry out justice and righteousness."

⁹ Then she gave the king four and a half tons of gold, a great quantity of spices, and precious stones. There never were such spices as those the queen of Sheba gave to King Solomon. ¹⁰ In addition, Hiram's servants and Solomon's servants who brought gold from Ophir also brought algum wood and precious stones. ¹¹ The king made the algum wood into walkways for the LORD's temple and for the king's palace and into lyres and harps for the singers. Never before had anything like them been seen in the land of Judah.

¹² King Solomon gave the queen of Sheba her every desire, whatever she asked—far more than she had brought the king. Then she, along with her servants, returned to her own country.

Solomon's Wealth

¹³ The weight of gold that came to Solomon annually was twenty-five tons, ¹⁴ besides what was brought by the merchants and traders. All the Arabian kings and governors of the land also brought gold and silver to Solomon.

¹⁵ King Solomon made two hundred large shields of hammered gold; 15 pounds of hammered gold went into each shield. ¹⁶ He made three hundred small shields of hammered gold; 7½ pounds of gold went into each shield. The king put them in the House of the Forest of Lebanon.

¹⁷ The king also made a large ivory throne and overlaid it with pure gold. ¹⁸ The throne had six steps; there was a footstool covered in gold for the throne, armrests on either side of the seat, and two lions standing beside the armrests. ¹⁹ Twelve lions were standing there on the six steps, one at each end. Nothing like it had ever been made in any other kingdom.

²⁰ All of King Solomon's drinking cups were gold, and all the utensils of the House of the Forest of Lebanon were pure gold. There was no silver, since it was considered as nothing in Solomon's time, ²¹ for the king's ships kept going to Tarshish with Hiram's servants, and once every three years the ships of Tarshish would arrive bearing gold, silver, ivory, apes, and peacocks.

²² King Solomon surpassed all the kings of the world in riches and wisdom. ²³ All the kings of the world wanted an audience with Solomon to hear the wisdom God had put in his heart. ²⁴ Each of them would bring his own gift—items of silver and gold, clothing, weapons, spices, and horses and mules—as an annual tribute.

²⁵ Solomon had four thousand stalls for horses and chariots, and twelve thousand horsemen. He stationed them in the chariot cities and with the king in Jerusalem. ²⁶ He ruled over all the kings from the Euphrates River to the land of the Philistines and as far as the border of Egypt. ²⁷ The

king made silver as common in Jerusalem as stones, and he made cedar as abundant as sycamore in the Judean foothills. ²⁸ They were bringing horses for Solomon from Egypt and from all the countries.

Solomon's Death

²⁹ The remaining events of Solomon's reign, from beginning to end, are written in the Events of the Prophet Nathan, the Prophecy of Ahijah the Shilonite, and the Visions of the Seer Iddo concerning Jeroboam son of Nebat. ³⁰ Solomon reigned in Jerusalem over all Israel for forty years. ³¹ Solomon rested with his ancestors and was buried in the city of his father David. His son Rehoboam became king in his place.

◆ GOING DEEPER

PSALM 72

A Prayer for the King
Of Solomon.

¹ God, give your justice to the king
and your righteousness to the king's son.
² He will judge your people with righteousness
and your afflicted ones with justice.
³ May the mountains bring well-being to the people
and the hills, righteousness.
⁴ May he vindicate the afflicted among the people,
help the poor,
and crush the oppressor.

⁵ May they fear you while the sun endures
and as long as the moon, throughout all generations.
⁶ May the king be like rain that falls on the cut grass,
like spring showers that water the earth.
⁷ May the righteous flourish in his days
and well-being abound
until the moon is no more.

⁸ May he rule from sea to sea
and from the Euphrates
to the ends of the earth.
⁹ May desert tribes kneel before him
and his enemies lick the dust.
¹⁰ May the kings of Tarshish
and the coasts and islands bring tribute,
the kings of Sheba and Seba offer gifts.
¹¹ Let all kings bow in homage to him,
all nations serve him.

¹² For he will rescue the poor who cry out
and the afflicted who have no helper.
¹³ He will have pity on the poor and helpless
and save the lives of the poor.
¹⁴ He will redeem them from oppression and violence,
for their lives are precious in his sight.

¹⁵ May he live long!
May gold from Sheba be given to him.
May prayer be offered for him continually,
and may he be blessed all day long.
¹⁶ May there be plenty of grain in the land;
may it wave on the tops of the mountains.
May its crops be like Lebanon.
May people flourish in the cities
like the grass of the field.
¹⁷ May his name endure forever;
as long as the sun shines,
may his fame increase.
May all nations be blessed by him
and call him blessed.

¹⁸ Blessed be the LORD God, the God of Israel,
who alone does wonders.
¹⁹ Blessed be his glorious name forever;
the whole earth is filled with his glory.
Amen and amen.
²⁰ The prayers of David son of Jesse are concluded.

God's People Divided

2 CHRONICLES 10-36

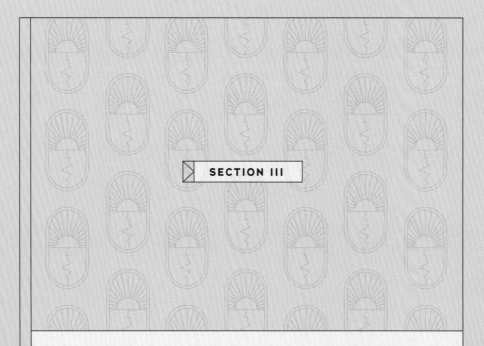

SECTION III

The final section of Chronicles details the time of the divided kingdoms: Israel, the northern kingdom, and Judah, the southern kingdom. These chapters focus mainly on the kings of the southern kingdom of Judah. The Chronicler points to the spiritual amnesia of Judah's people and leaders—forgetting who God is and their identity as God's people to instead worship other gods and neglect God's law. Despite a few upright kings who stood out among the rest, this section provides a look at the repeated pattern of disobedience that dominated Judah's division and road to exile.

Second Chronicles ends with a retelling of the people's return from exile to start a new era of rebuilding and restoration.

GOD'S
PEOPLE
DIVIDED

Rehoboam Abandons God's Law

2 CHRONICLES 10

The Kingdom Divided

¹ Then Rehoboam went to Shechem, for all Israel had gone to Shechem to make him king. ² When Jeroboam son of Nebat heard about it—for he was in Egypt where he had fled from King Solomon's presence—Jeroboam returned from Egypt. ³ So they summoned him. Then Jeroboam and all Israel came and spoke to Rehoboam: ⁴ "Your father made our yoke harsh. Therefore, lighten your father's harsh service and the heavy yoke he put on us, and we will serve you."

⁵ Rehoboam replied, "Return to me in three days." So the people left.

⁶ Then King Rehoboam consulted with the elders who had attended his father Solomon when he was alive, asking, "How do you advise me to respond to this people?"

⁷ They replied, "If you will be kind to this people and please them by speaking kind words to them, they will be your servants forever."

⁸ But he rejected the advice of the elders who had advised him, and he consulted with the young men who had grown up with him, the ones attending him. ⁹ He asked them, "What message do you advise we send back to this people who said to me, 'Lighten the yoke your father put on us'?"

[10] Then the young men who had grown up with him told him, "This is what you should say to the people who said to you, 'Your father made our yoke heavy, but you, make it lighter on us!' This is what you should say to them: 'My little finger is thicker than my father's waist! [11] Now therefore, my father burdened you with a heavy yoke, but I will add to your yoke; my father disciplined you with whips, but I, with barbed whips.'"

[12] So Jeroboam and all the people came to Rehoboam on the third day, just as the king had ordered, saying, "Return to me on the third day." [13] Then the king answered them harshly. King Rehoboam rejected the elders' advice [14] and spoke to them according to the young men's advice, saying, "My father made your yoke heavy, but I will add to it; my father disciplined you with whips, but I, with barbed whips."

[15] The king did not listen to the people because the turn of events came from God, in order that the LORD might carry out his word that he had spoken through Ahijah the Shilonite to Jeroboam son of Nebat.

[16] When all Israel saw that the king had not listened to them, the people answered the king:

> What portion do we have in David?
> We have no inheritance in the son of Jesse.
> Israel, each to your tent;
> David, look after your own house now!

So all Israel went to their tents. [17] But as for the Israelites living in the cities of Judah, Rehoboam reigned over them.

[18] Then King Rehoboam sent Hadoram, who was in charge of the forced labor, but the Israelites stoned him to death. However, King Rehoboam managed to get into his chariot to flee to Jerusalem. [19] Israel is in rebellion against the house of David until today.

2 CHRONICLES 11

Rehoboam in Jerusalem

[1] When Rehoboam arrived in Jerusalem, he mobilized the house of Judah and Benjamin—one hundred eighty thousand fit young soldiers—to fight against Israel to restore the reign to Rehoboam. [2] But the word of the LORD came to Shemaiah, the man of God: [3] "Say to Rehoboam son of Solomon, king of Judah, to all Israel in Judah and Benjamin, and to the rest of the people, [4] 'This is what the LORD says: You are not to march up and fight against your brothers. Each of you return home, for this incident has come from me.'"

So they listened to what the LORD said and turned back from going against Jeroboam.

Judah's King Rehoboam

[5] Rehoboam stayed in Jerusalem, and he fortified cities in Judah. [6] He built up Bethlehem, Etam, Tekoa, [7] Beth-zur, Soco, Adullam, [8] Gath, Mareshah, Ziph, [9] Adoraim, Lachish, Azekah, [10] Zorah, Aijalon, and Hebron, which are fortified cities in Judah and in Benjamin. [11] He strengthened their fortifications and put leaders in them with supplies of food, oil, and wine. [12] He also put large shields and spears in each and every city to make them very strong. So Judah and Benjamin were his.

[13] The priests and Levites from all their regions throughout Israel took their stand with Rehoboam, [14] for the Levites left their pasturelands and their possessions and went to Judah and Jerusalem, because Jeroboam and his sons refused to let them serve as priests of the LORD. [15] Jeroboam appointed his own priests for the high places, the goat-demons, and the golden calves he had made. [16] Those from every tribe of Israel who had determined in their hearts to seek the LORD their God followed the Levites to Jerusalem to sacrifice to the LORD, the God of their ancestors. [17] So they strengthened the kingdom of Judah and supported Rehoboam son of Solomon for three years, because they walked in the ways of David and Solomon for three years.

[18] Rehoboam married Mahalath, daughter of David's son Jerimoth and of Abihail daughter of Jesse's son Eliab. [19] She bore sons to him: Jeush, Shemariah, and Zaham. [20] After her, he married Maacah daughter of Absalom. She bore Abijah, Attai, Ziza, and Shelomith to him. [21] Rehoboam loved Maacah daughter of Absalom more than all his wives and concubines. He acquired eighteen wives and sixty

concubines and was the father of twenty-eight sons and sixty daughters.

²² Rehoboam appointed Abijah son of Maacah as chief, leader among his brothers, intending to make him king. ²³ Rehoboam also showed discernment by dispersing some of his sons to all the regions of Judah and Benjamin and to all the fortified cities. He gave them plenty of provisions and sought many wives for them.

2 CHRONICLES 12

Shishak's Invasion

¹ When Rehoboam had established his sovereignty and royal power, he abandoned the law of the LORD—he and all Israel with him. ² Because they were unfaithful to the LORD, in the fifth year of King Rehoboam, King Shishak of Egypt went to war against Jerusalem ³ with 1,200 chariots, 60,000 cavalrymen, and countless people who came with him from Egypt—Libyans, Sukkiim, and Cushites. ⁴ He captured the fortified cities of Judah and came as far as Jerusalem.

⁵ Then the prophet Shemaiah went to Rehoboam and the leaders of Judah who were gathered at Jerusalem because of Shishak. He said to them, "This is what the LORD says: You have abandoned me; therefore, I have abandoned you to Shishak."

⁶ So the leaders of Israel and the king humbled themselves and said, "The LORD is righteous."

⁷ When the LORD saw that they had humbled themselves, the LORD's message came to Shemaiah: "They have humbled themselves; I will not destroy them but will grant them a little deliverance. My wrath will not be poured out on Jerusalem through Shishak. ⁸ However, they will become his servants so that they may recognize the difference between serving me and serving the kingdoms of other lands."

⁹ So King Shishak of Egypt went to war against Jerusalem. He seized the treasuries of the LORD's temple and the treasuries of the royal palace. He took everything. He took the gold shields that Solomon had made. ¹⁰ King Rehoboam made bronze shields to replace them and committed them into the care of the captains of the guards who protected the entrance to the king's palace. ¹¹ Whenever the king entered the LORD's temple, the guards would carry the shields and take them back to the armory. ¹² When Rehoboam humbled himself, the LORD's anger turned away from him, and he did not destroy him completely. Besides that, conditions were good in Judah.

Rehoboam's Last Days

¹³ King Rehoboam established his royal power in Jerusalem. Rehoboam was forty-one years old when he became king, and he reigned seventeen years in Jerusalem, the city the LORD had chosen from all the tribes of Israel to put his name. Rehoboam's mother's name was Naamah the Ammonite.

¹⁴ Rehoboam did what was evil, because he did not determine in his heart to seek the LORD.

¹⁵ The events of Rehoboam's reign, from beginning to end, are written in the Events of the Prophet Shemaiah and of the Seer Iddo concerning genealogies. There was war between Rehoboam and Jeroboam throughout their reigns. ¹⁶ Rehoboam rested with his ancestors and was buried in the city of David. His son Abijah became king in his place.

GOING DEEPER

PROVERBS 10:17

The one who follows instruction is on the path to life, but the one who rejects correction goes astray.

Revival Under King Asa

2 CHRONICLES 13

Judah's King Abijah

¹ In the eighteenth year of Israel's King Jeroboam, Abijah became king over Judah, ² and he reigned three years in Jerusalem. His mother's name was Micaiah daughter of Uriel; she was from Gibeah.

There was war between Abijah and Jeroboam. ³ Abijah set his army of warriors in order with four hundred thousand fit young men. Jeroboam arranged his mighty army of eight hundred thousand fit young men in battle formation against him. ⁴ Then Abijah stood on Mount Zemaraim, which is in the hill country of Ephraim, and said, "Jeroboam and all Israel, hear me. ⁵ Don't you know that the LORD God of Israel gave the kingship over Israel to David and his descendants forever by a covenant of salt? ⁶ But Jeroboam son of Nebat, a servant of Solomon son of David, rose up and rebelled against his lord. ⁷ Then worthless and wicked men gathered around him to resist Rehoboam son of Solomon when Rehoboam was young, inexperienced, and unable to assert himself against them.

⁸ "And now you are saying you can assert yourselves against the LORD's kingdom, which is in the hand of one of David's sons. You are a vast number and have with you the golden calves that Jeroboam made for you as gods. ⁹ Didn't you banish the priests of the LORD, the descendants of Aaron and the Levites, and make your own priests like the peoples of other lands do? Whoever comes to ordain himself with a young bull and seven rams may become a priest of what are not gods.

¹⁰ "But as for us, the LORD is our God. We have not abandoned him; the priests ministering to the LORD are descendants of Aaron, and the Levites serve at their tasks.

¹¹ They offer a burnt offering and fragrant incense to the LORD every morning and every evening, and they set the rows of the Bread of the Presence on the ceremonially clean table. They light the lamps of the gold lampstand every evening. We are carrying out the requirements of the LORD our God, while you have abandoned him. ¹² Look, God and his priests are with us at our head. The trumpets are ready to sound the charge against you. Israelites, don't fight against the LORD God of your ancestors, for you will not succeed."

¹³ Now Jeroboam had sent an ambush around to advance from behind them. So they were in front of Judah, and the ambush was behind them. ¹⁴ Judah turned and discovered that the battle was in front of them and behind them, so they cried out to the LORD. Then the priests blew the trumpets, ¹⁵ and the men of Judah raised the battle cry. When the men of Judah raised the battle cry, God routed Jeroboam and all Israel before Abijah and Judah. ¹⁶ So the Israelites fled before Judah, and God handed them over to them. ¹⁷ Then Abijah and his people struck them with a mighty blow, and five hundred thousand fit young men of Israel were killed. ¹⁸ The Israelites were subdued at that time. The Judahites succeeded because they depended on the LORD, the God of their ancestors.

¹⁹ Abijah pursued Jeroboam and captured some cities from him: Bethel, Jeshanah, and Ephron, along with their surrounding villages. ²⁰ Jeroboam no longer retained his power during Abijah's reign; ultimately, the LORD struck him and he died.

²¹ However, Abijah grew strong, acquired fourteen wives, and fathered twenty-two sons and sixteen daughters. ²² The

rest of the events of Abijah's reign, along with his ways and his sayings, are written in the Writing of the Prophet Iddo.

2 CHRONICLES 14

¹ Abijah rested with his ancestors and was buried in the city of David. His son Asa became king in his place. During his reign the land experienced peace for ten years.

Judah's King Asa

² Asa did what was good and right in the sight of the LORD his God. ³ He removed the pagan altars and the high places. He shattered their sacred pillars and chopped down their Asherah poles. ⁴ He told the people of Judah to seek the LORD God of their ancestors and to carry out the instruction and the commands. ⁵ He also removed the high places and the shrines from all the cities of Judah, and the kingdom experienced peace under him.

⁶ Because the land experienced peace, Asa built fortified cities in Judah. No one made war with him in those days because the LORD gave him rest. ⁷ So he said to the people of Judah, "Let's build these cities and surround them with walls and towers, with doors and bars.

The land is still ours because we sought the LORD our God.

We sought him and he gave us rest on every side." So they built and succeeded.

The Cushite Invasion

⁸ Asa had an army of three hundred thousand from Judah bearing large shields and spears, and two hundred eighty thousand from Benjamin bearing regular shields and drawing the bow. All these were valiant warriors. ⁹ Then Zerah the Cushite came against them with an army of one million men and three hundred chariots. They came as far as Mareshah. ¹⁰ So Asa marched out against him and lined up in battle formation in Zephathah Valley at Mareshah.

¹¹ Then Asa cried out to the LORD his God, "LORD, there is no one besides you to help the mighty and those without strength. Help us, LORD our God, for we depend on you, and in your name we have come against this large army. LORD, you are our God. Do not let a mere mortal hinder you."

¹² So the LORD routed the Cushites before Asa and before Judah, and the Cushites fled. ¹³ Then Asa and the people who were with him pursued them as far as Gerar. The Cushites fell until they had no survivors, for they were crushed before the LORD and his army. So the people of Judah carried off a great supply of loot. ¹⁴ Then they attacked all the cities around Gerar because the terror of the LORD was on them. They

also plundered all the cities, since there was a great deal of plunder in them. ¹⁵ They also attacked the tents of the herdsmen and captured many sheep and camels. Then they returned to Jerusalem.

2 CHRONICLES 15

Revival Under Asa

¹ The Spirit of God came on Azariah son of Oded. ² So he went out to meet Asa and said to him, "Asa and all Judah and Benjamin, hear me. The LORD is with you when you are with him. If you seek him, he will be found by you, but if you abandon him, he will abandon you. ³ For many years Israel has been without the true God, without a teaching priest, and without instruction, ⁴ but when they turned to the LORD God of Israel in their distress and sought him, he was found by them. ⁵ In those times there was no peace for those who went about their daily activities because the residents of the lands had many conflicts. ⁶ Nation was crushed by nation and city by city, for God troubled them with every possible distress. ⁷ But as for you, be strong; don't give up, for your work has a reward."

⁸ When Asa heard these words and the prophecy of Azariah son of Oded the prophet, he took courage and removed the abhorrent idols from the whole land of Judah and Benjamin and from the cities he had captured in the hill country of Ephraim. He renovated the altar of the LORD that was in front of the portico of the LORD's temple. ⁹ Then he gathered all Judah and Benjamin, as well as those from the tribes of Ephraim, Manasseh, and Simeon who were residing among them, for they had defected to him from Israel in great numbers when they saw that the LORD his God was with him.

¹⁰ They were gathered in Jerusalem in the third month of the fifteenth year of Asa's reign. ¹¹ At that time they sacrificed to the LORD seven hundred cattle and seven thousand sheep and goats from all the plunder they had brought. ¹² Then they entered into a covenant to seek the LORD God of their ancestors with all their heart and all their soul. ¹³ Whoever would not seek the LORD God of Israel would be put to death, young or old, man or woman. ¹⁴ They took an oath to the LORD in a loud voice, with shouting, with trumpets, and with rams' horns. ¹⁵ All Judah rejoiced over the oath, for they had sworn it wholeheartedly. They had sought him with all sincerity, and he was found by them. So the LORD gave them rest on every side.

¹⁶ King Asa also removed Maacah, his grandmother, from being queen mother because she had made an obscene image of Asherah. Asa chopped down her obscene image, then crushed it and burned it in the Kidron Valley. ¹⁷ The high places were not taken away from Israel; nevertheless, Asa was wholeheartedly devoted his entire life. ¹⁸ He brought his father's consecrated gifts and his own consecrated gifts into God's temple: silver, gold, and utensils.

¹⁹ There was no war until the thirty-fifth year of Asa's reign.

2 CHRONICLES 16

Asa's Treaty with Aram

[1] In the thirty-sixth year of Asa, Israel's King Baasha went to war against Judah. He built Ramah in order to keep anyone from leaving or coming to King Asa of Judah. [2] So Asa brought out the silver and gold from the treasuries of the LORD's temple and the royal palace and sent it to Aram's King Ben-hadad, who lived in Damascus, saying, [3] "There's a treaty between me and you, between my father and your father. Look, I have sent you silver and gold. Go break your treaty with Israel's King Baasha so that he will withdraw from me."

[4] Ben-hadad listened to King Asa and sent the commanders of his armies to the cities of Israel. They attacked Ijon, Dan, Abel-maim, and all the storage cities of Naphtali. [5] When Baasha heard about it, he quit building Ramah and stopped his work. [6] Then King Asa brought all Judah, and they carried away the stones of Ramah and the timbers Baasha had built it with. Then he built Geba and Mizpah with them.

Hanani's Rebuke of Asa

[7] At that time, the seer Hanani came to King Asa of Judah and said to him, "Because you depended on the king of Aram and have not depended on the LORD your God, the army of the king of Aram has escaped from you. [8] Were not the Cushites and Libyans a vast army with many chariots and horsemen? When you depended on the LORD, he handed them over to you. [9] For the eyes of the LORD roam throughout the earth to show himself strong for those who are wholeheartedly devoted to him. You have been foolish in this matter. Therefore, you will have wars from now on." [10] Asa was enraged with the seer and put him in prison because of his anger over this. And Asa mistreated some of the people at that time.

Asa's Death

[11] Note that the events of Asa's reign, from beginning to end, are written in the Book of the Kings of Judah and Israel. [12] In the thirty-ninth year of his reign, Asa developed a disease in his feet, and his disease became increasingly severe. Yet even in his disease he didn't seek the LORD but

only the physicians. [13] Asa rested with his ancestors; he died in the forty-first year of his reign. [14] He was buried in his own tomb that he had made for himself in the city of David. They laid him out in a coffin that was full of spices and various mixtures of prepared ointments; then they made a great fire in his honor.

🔖 GOING DEEPER

JOHN 14:21

"The one who has my commands and keeps them is the one who loves me. And the one who loves me will be loved by my Father. I also will love him and will reveal myself to him."

Grace Day

But Christ has appeared as a high priest of the good things that have come. In the greater and more perfect tabernacle not made with hands (that is, not of this creation), he entered the most holy place once for all time, not by the blood of goats and calves, but by his own blood, having obtained eternal redemption.

Take this day to catch up on your reading, pray, and rest in the presence of the Lord.

HEBREWS 9:11–12

Weekly Truth

DAY 28

WEEK 4

Scripture is God-breathed and true. When we memorize it, we carry His Word with us wherever we go.

See tips for memorizing Scripture on page 240.

This week we will commit to memory David's prayer of blessing in 1 Chronicles 29:11–13. Give God thanks and praise as you meditate on and memorize verse 13.

Yours, LORD, is the greatness and the power and the glory and the splendor and the majesty, for everything in the heavens and on earth belongs to you. Yours, LORD, is the kingdom, and you are exalted as head over all. Riches and honor come from you, and you are the ruler of everything. Power and might are in your hand, and it is in your hand to make great and to give strength to all. Now therefore, our God, we give you thanks and praise your glorious name.

1 CHRONICLES 29:11-13

GOD'S
PEOPLE
DIVIDED

Judah's King Jehoshaphat

WEEK 5

DAY 29

2 CHRONICLES 17

Judah's King Jehoshaphat

¹ His son Jehoshaphat became king in his place and strengthened himself against Israel. ² He stationed troops in every fortified city of Judah and set garrisons in the land of Judah and in the cities of Ephraim that his father Asa had captured.

³ Now the LORD was with Jehoshaphat because he walked in the former ways of his ancestor David. He did not seek the Baals ⁴ but sought the God of his father and walked by his commands, not according to the practices of Israel. ⁵ So the LORD established the kingdom in his hand. Then all Judah brought him tribute, and he had riches and honor in abundance. ⁶ He took great pride in the LORD's ways, and he again removed the high places and Asherah poles from Judah.

Jehoshaphat's Educational Plan

⁷ In the third year of his reign, Jehoshaphat sent his officials—Ben-hail, Obadiah, Zechariah, Nethanel, and Micaiah—to teach in the cities of Judah. ⁸ The Levites with them were Shemaiah, Nethaniah, Zebadiah, Asahel, Shemiramoth, Jehonathan, Adonijah, Tobijah, and Tob-adonijah; the priests, Elishama and Jehoram, were with these Levites. ⁹ They taught throughout Judah, having the book of the LORD's instruction with them. They went throughout the towns of Judah and taught the people.

¹⁰ The terror of the LORD was on all the kingdoms of the lands that surrounded Judah, so they didn't fight against Jehoshaphat. ¹¹ Some of the Philistines also brought gifts and silver as tribute to Jehoshaphat, and the Arabs brought him flocks: 7,700 rams and 7,700 male goats.

Jehoshaphat's Military Might

¹² Jehoshaphat grew stronger and stronger. He built fortresses and storage cities in Judah ¹³ and carried out great works in the towns of Judah. He had fighting men, valiant warriors, in Jerusalem. ¹⁴ These are their numbers according to their ancestral families. For Judah, the commanders of thousands:

Adnah the commander and three hundred thousand valiant warriors with him;

¹⁵ next to him, Jehohanan the commander and two hundred eighty thousand with him;

¹⁶ next to him, Amasiah son of Zichri, the volunteer of the LORD, and two hundred thousand valiant warriors with him;

¹⁷ from Benjamin, Eliada, a valiant warrior, and two hundred thousand with him armed with bow and shield;

¹⁸ next to him, Jehozabad and one hundred eighty thousand with him equipped for war.

¹⁹ These were the ones who served the king, besides those he stationed in the fortified cities throughout all Judah.

2 CHRONICLES 18

Jehoshaphat's Alliance with Ahab

¹ Now Jehoshaphat had riches and honor in abundance, and he made an alliance with Ahab through marriage. ² Then after some years, he went down to visit Ahab in Samaria. Ahab slaughtered many sheep, goats, and cattle for him and for the people who were with him, and he persuaded him to attack Ramoth-gilead, ³ for Israel's King Ahab asked Judah's King Jehoshaphat, "Will you go with me to Ramoth-gilead?"

He replied to him, "I am as you are, my people as your people; we will be with you in the battle." ⁴ But Jehoshaphat said to the king of Israel, "First, please ask what the LORD's will is."

⁵ So the king of Israel gathered the prophets, four hundred men, and asked them, "Should we go to Ramoth-gilead for war or should I refrain?"

They replied, "March up, and God will hand it over to the king."

⁶ But Jehoshaphat asked, "Isn't there a prophet of the LORD here anymore? Let's ask him."

⁷ The king of Israel said to Jehoshaphat, "There is still one man who can inquire of the Lord, but I hate him because he never prophesies good about me, but only disaster. He is Micaiah son of Imlah."

"The king shouldn't say that," Jehoshaphat replied.

⁸ So the king of Israel called an officer and said, "Hurry and get Micaiah son of Imlah!"

⁹ Now the king of Israel and King Jehoshaphat of Judah, clothed in royal attire, were each sitting on his own throne. They were sitting on the threshing floor at the entrance to Samaria's gate, and all the prophets were prophesying in front of them. ¹⁰ Then Zedekiah son of Chenaanah made iron horns and said, "This is what the Lord says: You will gore the Arameans with these until they are finished off." ¹¹ And all the prophets were prophesying the same, saying, "March up to Ramoth-gilead and succeed, for the Lord will hand it over to the king."

Micaiah's Message of Defeat

¹² The messenger who went to call Micaiah instructed him, "Look, the words of the prophets are unanimously favorable for the king. So let your words be like theirs, and speak favorably."

¹³ But Micaiah said, "As the Lord lives, I will say whatever my God says."

¹⁴ So he went to the king, and the king asked him, "Micaiah, should we go to Ramoth-gilead for war, or should I refrain?"

Micaiah said, "March up and succeed, for they will be handed over to you."

¹⁵ But the king said to him, "How many times must I make you swear not to tell me anything but the truth in the name of the Lord?"

¹⁶ So Micaiah said:

I saw all Israel scattered on the hills
like sheep without a shepherd.
And the Lord said,

"They have no master;
let each return home in peace."

¹⁷ So the king of Israel said to Jehoshaphat, "Didn't I tell you he never prophesies good about me, but only disaster?"

¹⁸ Then Micaiah said, "Therefore, hear the word of the Lord. I saw the Lord sitting on his throne, and the whole heavenly army was standing at his right hand and at his left hand. ¹⁹ And the Lord said, 'Who will entice King Ahab of Israel to march up and fall at Ramoth-gilead?' So one was saying this and another was saying that.

²⁰ "Then a spirit came forward, stood before the Lord, and said, 'I will entice him.'

"The Lord asked him, 'How?'

²¹ "So he said, 'I will go and become a lying spirit in the mouth of all his prophets.'

"Then he said, 'You will entice him and also prevail. Go and do that.'

²² "Now, you see, the Lord has put a lying spirit into the mouth of these prophets of yours, and the Lord has pronounced disaster against you."

²³ Then Zedekiah son of Chenaanah came up, hit Micaiah on the cheek, and demanded, "Which way did the spirit from the Lord leave me to speak to you?"

²⁴ Micaiah replied, "You will soon see when you go to hide in an inner chamber on that day."

²⁵ Then the king of Israel ordered, "Take Micaiah and return him to Amon, the governor of the city, and to Joash, the king's son, ²⁶ and say, 'This is what the king says: Put this guy in prison and feed him only a little bread and water until I come back safely.'"

²⁷ But Micaiah said, "If you ever return safely, the Lord has not spoken through me." Then he said, "Listen, all you people!"

Ahab's Death

²⁸ Then the king of Israel and Judah's King Jehoshaphat went up to Ramoth-gilead. ²⁹ But the king of Israel said to Jehoshaphat, "I will disguise myself and go into battle, but you wear your royal attire." So the king of Israel disguised himself, and they went into battle.

³⁰ Now the king of Aram had ordered his chariot commanders, "Do not fight with anyone at all except the king of Israel."

³¹ When the chariot commanders saw Jehoshaphat, they shouted, "He must be the king of Israel!" So they turned to attack him, but Jehoshaphat cried out and the Lord helped him. God drew them away from him. ³² When the chariot commanders saw that he was not the king of Israel, they turned back from pursuing him.

³³ But a man drew his bow without taking special aim and struck the king of Israel through the joints of his armor. So he said to the charioteer, "Turn around and take me out of the battle, for I am badly wounded!" ³⁴ The battle raged throughout that day, and the king of Israel propped himself up in his chariot facing the Arameans until evening. Then he died at sunset.

◥ GOING DEEPER

PSALM 33:16–22

¹⁶ A king is not saved by a large army;
a warrior will not be rescued by great strength.
¹⁷ The horse is a false hope for safety;
it provides no escape by its great power.

¹⁸ But look, the Lord keeps his eye on those who fear him—
those who depend on his faithful love
¹⁹ to rescue them from death
and to keep them alive in famine.

²⁰ We wait for the Lord;
he is our help and shield.
²¹ For our hearts rejoice in him
because we trust in his holy name.
²² May your faithful love rest on us, Lord,
for we put our hope in you.

King Jehoshaphat's Reforms

2 CHRONICLES 19

Jehu's Rebuke of Jehoshaphat

¹ King Jehoshaphat of Judah returned to his home in Jerusalem in peace. ² Then Jehu son of the seer Hanani went out to confront him and said to King Jehoshaphat, "Do you help the wicked and love those who hate the LORD? Because of this, the LORD's wrath is on you. ³ However, some good is found in you, for you have eradicated the Asherah poles from the land and have determined in your heart to seek God."

Jehoshaphat's Reforms

⁴ Jehoshaphat lived in Jerusalem, and once again he went out among the people from Beer-sheba to the hill country of Ephraim and brought them back to the LORD, the God of their ancestors. ⁵ He appointed judges in all the fortified cities of the land of Judah, city by city. ⁶ Then he said to the judges, "Consider what you are doing, for you do not judge for a man, but for the LORD, who is with you in the matter of judgment. ⁷ And now, may the terror of the LORD be on you.

Watch what you do, for there is no injustice or partiality or taking bribes with the LORD our God."

⁸ Jehoshaphat also appointed in Jerusalem some of the Levites and priests and some of the Israelite family heads for deciding the LORD's will and for settling disputes of the residents of Jerusalem. ⁹ He commanded them, saying, "In the fear of the LORD, with integrity, and wholeheartedly, you are to do the following: ¹⁰ For every dispute that comes to you from your brothers who dwell in their cities—whether it regards differences of bloodguilt, law, commandment, statutes, or judgments—you are to warn them, so they will not incur guilt before the LORD and wrath will not come on you and your brothers. Do this, and you will not incur guilt.

¹¹ "Note that Amariah, the chief priest, is over you in all matters related to the LORD, and Zebadiah son of Ishmael, the ruler of the house of Judah, in all matters related to the king, and the Levites are officers in your presence. Be strong; may the LORD be with those who do what is good."

2 CHRONICLES 20

War Against Eastern Enemies

¹ After this, the Moabites and Ammonites, together with some of the Meunites, came to fight against Jehoshaphat. ² People came and told Jehoshaphat, "A vast number from beyond the Dead Sea and from Edom has come to fight against you; they are already in Hazazon-tamar" (that is, En-gedi). ³ Jehoshaphat was afraid, and he resolved to seek the LORD. Then he proclaimed a fast for all Judah, ⁴ who gathered to seek the LORD. They even came from all the cities of Judah to seek him.

Jehoshaphat's Prayer

⁵ Then Jehoshaphat stood in the assembly of Judah and Jerusalem in the LORD's temple before the new courtyard. ⁶ He said:

LORD, God of our ancestors, are you not the God who is in heaven, and do you not rule over all the kingdoms of the nations? Power and might are in your hand, and no one can stand against you. 7 Are you not our God who drove out the inhabitants of this land before your people Israel and who gave it forever to the descendants of Abraham your friend? 8 They have lived in the land and have built you a sanctuary in it for your name and have said, 9 "If disaster comes on us—sword or judgment, pestilence or famine—we will stand before this temple and before you, for your name is in this temple. We will cry out to you because of our distress, and you will hear and deliver."

10 Now here are the Ammonites, Moabites, and the inhabitants of Mount Seir. You did not let Israel invade them when Israel came out of the land of Egypt, but Israel turned away from them and did not destroy them. 11 Look how they repay us by coming to drive us out of your possession that you gave us as an inheritance. 12 Our God, will you not judge them? For we are powerless before this vast number that comes to fight against us. We do not know what to do, but we look to you.

God's Answer

13 All Judah was standing before the LORD with their dependents, their wives, and their children. 14 In the middle of the congregation, the Spirit of the LORD came on Jahaziel (son of Zechariah, son of Benaiah, son of Jeiel, son of Mattaniah, a Levite from Asaph's descendants), 15 and he said, "Listen carefully, all Judah and you inhabitants of Jerusalem, and King Jehoshaphat. This is what the LORD says: 'Do not be afraid or discouraged because of this vast number, for the battle is not yours, but God's. 16 Tomorrow, go down against them. You will see them coming up the Ascent of Ziz, and you will find them at the end of the valley facing the Wilderness of Jeruel. 17 You do not have to fight this battle. Position yourselves, stand still, and see the salvation of the LORD. He is with you, Judah and Jerusalem. Do not be afraid or discouraged. Tomorrow, go out to face them, for the LORD is with you.'"

18 Then Jehoshaphat knelt low with his face to the ground, and all Judah and the inhabitants of Jerusalem fell down before the LORD to worship him. 19 Then the Levites from the sons of the Kohathites and the Korahites stood up to praise the LORD God of Israel shouting loudly.

Victory and Plunder

20 In the morning they got up early and went out to the wilderness of Tekoa. As they were about to go out, Jehoshaphat stood and said, "Hear me, Judah and you inhabitants of Jerusalem. Believe in the LORD your God, and you will be established; believe in his prophets, and you will succeed." 21 Then he consulted with the people and appointed some to sing for the LORD and some to praise the splendor of his holiness. When they went out in front of the armed forces, they kept singing:

Give thanks to the LORD,
for his faithful love endures forever.

22 The moment they began their shouts and praises, the LORD set an ambush against the Ammonites, Moabites, and the inhabitants of Mount Seir who came to fight against Judah, and they were defeated. 23 The Ammonites and Moabites turned against the inhabitants of Mount Seir and completely annihilated them. When they had finished with the inhabitants of Seir, they helped destroy each other.

24 When Judah came to a place overlooking the wilderness, they looked for the large army, but there were only corpses lying on the ground; nobody had escaped. 25 Then Jehoshaphat and his people went to gather the plunder. They found among them an abundance of goods on the bodies and valuable items. So they stripped them until nobody could carry any more. They were gathering the plunder for three days because there was so much. 26 They assembled in the Valley of Beracah on the fourth day, for there they blessed the LORD. Therefore, that place is still called the Valley of Beracah today.

27 Then all the men of Judah and Jerusalem turned back with Jehoshaphat their leader, returning joyfully to Jerusalem, for the LORD enabled them to rejoice over their enemies. 28 So they came into Jerusalem to the LORD's temple with harps, lyres, and trumpets.

29 The terror of God was on all the kingdoms of the lands when they heard that the LORD had fought against the enemies of Israel.

³⁰ Then Jehoshaphat's kingdom was quiet, for his God gave him rest on every side.

NOTES

Summary of Jehoshaphat's Reign

³¹ Jehoshaphat became king over Judah. He was thirty-five years old when he became king, and he reigned twenty-five years in Jerusalem. His mother's name was Azubah daughter of Shilhi. ³² He walked in the ways of Asa his father; he did not turn away from it but did what was right in the LORD's sight. ³³ However, the high places were not taken away; the people had not yet set their hearts on the God of their ancestors.

³⁴ The rest of the events of Jehoshaphat's reign from beginning to end are written in the Events of Jehu son of Hanani, which is recorded in the Book of Israel's Kings.

Jehoshaphat's Fleet of Ships

³⁵ After this, Judah's King Jehoshaphat made an alliance with Israel's King Ahaziah, who was guilty of wrongdoing. ³⁶ Jehoshaphat formed an alliance with him to make ships to go to Tarshish, and they made the ships in Ezion-geber. ³⁷ Then Eliezer son of Dodavahu of Mareshah prophesied against Jehoshaphat, saying, "Because you formed an alliance with Ahaziah, the LORD has broken up what you have made." So the ships were wrecked and were not able to go to Tarshish.

2 CHRONICLES 21:1

Jehoram Becomes King over Judah

Jehoshaphat rested with his ancestors and was buried with his ancestors in the city of David. His son Jehoram became king in his place.

GOING DEEPER

EZRA 8:21–23

Preparing to Return

²¹ I proclaimed a fast by the Ahava River, so that we might humble ourselves before our God and ask him for a safe journey for us, our dependents, and all our possessions. ²² I did this because I was ashamed to ask the king for infantry and cavalry to protect us from enemies during the journey, since we had told him, "The hand of our God is gracious to all who seek him, but his fierce anger is against all who abandon him." ²³ So we fasted and pleaded with our God about this, and he was receptive to our prayer.

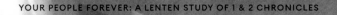

YOUR PEOPLE FOREVER: A LENTEN STUDY OF 1 & 2 CHRONICLES

Be it ours to remember the lovingkindness of the Lord, and to rehearse his deeds of grace. Let us open the volume of recollection which is so richly illuminated with memorials of mercy, and we shall soon be happy.

C. H. SPURGEON

King Jehoram Leads Judah Astray

2 CHRONICLES 21:2–20

[2] He had brothers, sons of Jehoshaphat: Azariah, Jehiel, Zechariah, Azariah, Michael, and Shephatiah; all these were the sons of King Jehoshaphat of Judah. [3] Their father had given them many gifts of silver, gold, and valuable things, along with fortified cities in Judah, but he gave the kingdom to Jehoram because he was the firstborn. [4] When Jehoram had established himself over his father's kingdom, he strengthened his position by killing with the sword all his brothers as well as some of the princes of Israel.

Judah's King Jehoram

[5] Jehoram was thirty-two years old when he became king, and he reigned eight years in Jerusalem. [6] He walked in the ways of the kings of Israel, as the house of Ahab had done, for Ahab's daughter was his wife. He did what was evil in the LORD's sight, [7] but for the sake of the covenant the LORD had made with David, he was unwilling to destroy the house of David since the LORD had promised to give a lamp to David and to his sons forever.

[8] During Jehoram's reign, Edom rebelled against Judah's control and appointed their own king. [9] So Jehoram crossed into Edom with his commanders and all his chariots. Then at night he set out to attack the Edomites who had surrounded him and the chariot commanders. [10] And now Edom is still in rebellion against Judah's control today. Libnah also rebelled at that time

against his control because he had abandoned the Lord, the God of his ancestors. ¹¹ Jehoram also built high places in the hills of Judah, and he caused the inhabitants of Jerusalem to prostitute themselves, and he led Judah astray.

Elijah's Letter to Jehoram

¹² Then a letter came to Jehoram from the prophet Elijah, saying:

This is what the Lord, the God of your ancestor David says: "Because you have not walked in the ways of your father Jehoshaphat or in the ways of King Asa of Judah ¹³ but have walked in the ways of the kings of Israel, have caused Judah and the inhabitants of Jerusalem to prostitute themselves like the house of Ahab prostituted itself, and also have killed your brothers, your father's family, who were better than you, ¹⁴ the Lord is now about to strike your people, your sons, your wives, and all your possessions with a horrible affliction. ¹⁵ You yourself will be struck with many illnesses, including a disease of the intestines, until your intestines come out day after day because of the disease."

Jehoram's Last Days

¹⁶ The Lord roused the spirit of the Philistines and the Arabs who lived near the Cushites to attack Jehoram. ¹⁷ So they went to war against Judah and invaded it. They carried off all the possessions found in the king's palace and also his sons and wives; not a son was left to him except Jehoahaz, his youngest son.

¹⁸ After all these things, the Lord afflicted him in his intestines with an incurable disease. ¹⁹ This continued day after day until two full years passed. Then his intestines came out because of his disease, and he died from severe illnesses. But his people did not hold a fire in his honor like the fire in honor of his predecessors.

²⁰ Jehoram was thirty-two years old when he became king; he reigned eight years in Jerusalem. He died to no one's regret and was buried in the city of David but not in the tombs of the kings.

2 CHRONICLES 22

Judah's King Ahaziah

¹ Then the inhabitants of Jerusalem made Ahaziah, his youngest son, king in his place, because the troops that had come with the Arabs to the camp had killed all the older sons. So Ahaziah son of Jehoram became king of Judah. ² Ahaziah was twenty-two years old when he became king, and he reigned one year in Jerusalem. His mother's name was Athaliah, granddaughter of Omri.

³ He walked in the ways of the house of Ahab, for his mother gave him evil advice. ⁴ So he did what was evil in the Lord's sight like the house of Ahab, for they were

his advisers after the death of his father, to his destruction. ⁵ He also followed their advice and went with Joram son of Israel's King Ahab to fight against King Hazael of Aram, in Ramoth-gilead. The Arameans wounded Joram, ⁶ so he returned to Jezreel to recover from the wounds they inflicted on him in Ramoth-gilead when he fought against King Hazael of Aram. Then Judah's King Ahaziah son of Jehoram went down to Jezreel to visit Joram son of Ahab since Joram was ill.

⁷ Ahaziah's downfall came from God when he went to Joram. When Ahaziah arrived, he went out with Joram to meet Jehu son of Nimshi, whom the LORD had anointed to destroy the house of Ahab. ⁸ So when Jehu executed judgment on the house of Ahab, he found the rulers of Judah and the sons of Ahaziah's brothers who were serving Ahaziah, and he killed them. ⁹ Then Jehu looked for Ahaziah, and Jehu's soldiers captured him (he was hiding in Samaria). So they brought Ahaziah to Jehu, and they killed him. The soldiers buried him, for they said, "He is the grandson of Jehoshaphat who sought the LORD with all his heart." So no one from the house of Ahaziah had the strength to rule the kingdom.

Athaliah Usurps the Throne

¹⁰ When Athaliah, Ahaziah's mother, saw that her son was dead, she proceeded to annihilate all the royal heirs of the house of Judah. ¹¹ Jehoshabeath, the king's daughter, rescued Joash son of Ahaziah from the king's sons who were being killed and put him and the one who nursed him in a bedroom. Now Jehoshabeath was the daughter of King Jehoram and the wife of the priest Jehoiada. Since she was Ahaziah's sister, she hid Joash from Athaliah so that she did not kill him. ¹² He was hiding with them in God's temple for six years while Athaliah reigned over the land.

🔖 GOING DEEPER

DEUTERONOMY 10:12–14

What God Requires

¹² And now, Israel, what does the LORD your God ask of you except to fear the LORD your God by walking in all his ways, to love him, and to worship the LORD your God with all your heart and all your soul?

¹³ Keep the LORD's commands and statutes I am giving you today, for your own good. ¹⁴ The heavens, indeed the highest heavens, belong to the LORD your God, as does the earth and everything in it.

GOD'S
PEOPLE
DIVIDED

King Joash's Apostasy

Athaliah Overthrown

¹ Then, in the seventh year, Jehoiada summoned his courage and took the commanders of hundreds into a covenant with him: Azariah son of Jeroham, Ishmael son of Jehohanan, Azariah son of Obed, Maaseiah son of Adaiah, and Elishaphat son of Zichri. ² They made a circuit throughout Judah. They gathered the Levites from all the cities of Judah and the family heads of Israel, and they came to Jerusalem.

³ Then the whole assembly made a covenant with the king in God's temple. Jehoiada said to them, "Here is the king's son! He will reign, just as the Lord promised concerning David's sons. ⁴ This is what you are to do: a third of you, priests and Levites who are coming on duty on the Sabbath, are to be gatekeepers. ⁵ A third are to be at the king's palace, and a third are to be at the Foundation Gate, and all the troops will be in the courtyards of the Lord's temple. ⁶ No one is to enter the Lord's temple but the priests and those Levites who serve; they may enter because they are holy, but all the people are to obey the requirement of the Lord. ⁷ The Levites are to completely surround the king with weapons in hand. Anyone who enters the temple is to be put to death. Accompany the king in all his daily tasks."

⁸ So the commanders of hundreds did everything the priest Jehoiada commanded. They each brought their men—those coming on duty on the Sabbath and those going off duty on the Sabbath—for the priest Jehoiada did not release the divisions. ⁹ The priest Jehoiada gave to the commanders of hundreds King David's spears, shields, and quivers that were in God's temple. ¹⁰ Then he stationed all the troops with their weapons in hand surrounding the king—from the right side of the temple to the left side, by the altar and by the temple.

¹¹ They brought out the king's son, put the crown on him, gave him the testimony, and made him king. Jehoiada and his sons anointed him and cried, "Long live the king!"

¹² When Athaliah heard the noise from the troops, the guards, and those praising the king, she went to the troops in the Lord's temple. ¹³ As she looked, there was the king standing by his pillar at the entrance. The commanders and the trumpeters were by the king, and all the people of the land were rejoicing and blowing trumpets while the singers with musical instruments were leading the praise. Athaliah tore her clothes and screamed, "Treason! Treason!"

¹⁴ Then the priest Jehoiada sent out the commanders of hundreds, those in charge of the army, saying, "Take her out between the ranks, and put anyone who follows her to death by the sword," for the priest had said, "Don't put her to death in the Lord's temple." ¹⁵ So they arrested her, and she went by the entrance of the Horse Gate to the king's palace, where they put her to death.

Jehoiada's Reforms

¹⁶ Then Jehoiada made a covenant between himself, the king, and the people that they would be the Lord's people. ¹⁷ So all the people went to the temple of Baal and tore it down. They smashed its altars and images and killed Mattan, the priest of Baal, at the altars.

¹⁸ Then Jehoiada put the oversight of the Lord's temple into the hands of the Levitical priests, whom David had appointed over the Lord's temple, to offer burnt offerings to the Lord as it is written in the law of Moses, with rejoicing and song

ordained by David. [19] He stationed gatekeepers at the gates of the LORD's temple so that nothing unclean could enter for any reason. [20] Then he took with him the commanders of hundreds, the nobles, the governors of the people, and all the people of the land and brought the king down from the LORD's temple. They entered the king's palace through the Upper Gate and seated the king on the throne of the kingdom. [21] All the people of the land rejoiced, and the city was quiet, for they had put Athaliah to death by the sword.

2 CHRONICLES 24

Judah's King Joash

[1] Joash was seven years old when he became king, and he reigned forty years in Jerusalem. His mother's name was Zibiah; she was from Beer-sheba. [2] Throughout the time of the priest Jehoiada, Joash did what was right in the LORD's sight. [3] Jehoiada acquired two wives for him, and he was the father of sons and daughters.

Repairing the Temple

[4] Afterward, Joash took it to heart to renovate the LORD's temple. [5] So he gathered the priests and Levites and said, "Go out to the cities of Judah and collect silver from all Israel to repair the temple of your God as needed year by year, and do it quickly."

However, the Levites did not hurry. [6] So the king called Jehoiada the high priest and said, "Why haven't you required the Levites to bring from Judah and Jerusalem the tax imposed by the LORD's servant Moses and the assembly of Israel for the tent of the testimony? [7] For the sons of that wicked Athaliah broke into the LORD's temple and even used the sacred things of the LORD's temple for the Baals."

[8] At the king's command a chest was made and placed outside the gate of the LORD's temple. [9] Then a proclamation was issued in Judah and Jerusalem that the tax God's servant Moses imposed on Israel in the wilderness be brought to the LORD. [10] All the leaders and all the people rejoiced, brought the tax, and put it in the chest until it was full. [11] Whenever the chest was brought by the Levites to the king's overseers,

and when they saw that there was a large amount of silver, the king's secretary and the high priest's deputy came and emptied the chest, picked it up, and returned it to its place. They did this daily and gathered the silver in abundance. [12] Then the king and Jehoiada gave it to those in charge of the labor on the LORD's temple, who were hiring stonecutters and carpenters to renovate the LORD's temple, also blacksmiths and coppersmiths to repair the LORD's temple.

[13] The workmen did their work, and through them the repairs progressed. They restored God's temple to its specifications and reinforced it. [14] When they finished, they presented the rest of the silver to the king and Jehoiada, who made articles for the LORD's temple with it—articles for ministry and for making burnt offerings, and ladles and articles of gold and silver. They regularly offered burnt offerings in the LORD's temple throughout Jehoiada's life.

Joash's Apostasy

[15] Jehoiada died when he was old and full of days; he was 130 years old at his death. [16] He was buried in the city of David with the kings because he had done what was good in Israel with respect to God and his temple.

[17] However, after Jehoiada died, the rulers of Judah came and paid homage to the king. Then the king listened to them, [18] and they abandoned the temple of the LORD, the God of their ancestors, and served the Asherah poles and the idols. So there was wrath against Judah and Jerusalem for this guilt of theirs. [19] Nevertheless, he sent them prophets to bring them back to the LORD; they admonished them, but the people would not listen.

[20] The Spirit of God enveloped Zechariah son of Jehoiada the priest. He stood above the people and said to them, "This is what God says,

'Why are you transgressing the LORD's commands so that you do not prosper? Because you have abandoned the LORD, he has abandoned you.'"

[21] But they conspired against him and stoned him at the king's command in the courtyard of the LORD's temple. [22] King Joash didn't remember the kindness that Zechariah's father Jehoiada had extended to him, but killed his son. While he was dying, he said, "May the LORD see and demand an account."

Aramean Invasion of Judah

[23] At the turn of the year, an Aramean army attacked Joash. They entered Judah and Jerusalem and destroyed all the leaders of the people among them and sent all the plunder to the king of Damascus. [24] Although the Aramean army came with only a few men, the LORD handed over a vast army to them because the people of Judah had abandoned the LORD, the God of their ancestors. So they executed judgment on Joash.

Joash Assassinated

[25] When the Arameans saw that Joash had many wounds, they left him. His servants conspired against him, and killed him on his bed, because he had shed the blood of the sons of the priest Jehoiada. So he died, and they buried him in the city of David, but they did not bury him in the tombs of the kings.

[26] Those who conspired against him were Zabad, son of the Ammonite woman Shimeath, and Jehozabad, son of the Moabite woman Shimrith. [27] The accounts concerning his sons, the many divine pronouncements about him, and the restoration of God's temple are recorded in the Writing of the Book of the Kings. His son Amaziah became king in his place.

◗ GOING DEEPER

PSALM 2:10-12

[10] So now, kings, be wise;
receive instruction, you judges of the earth.
[11] Serve the LORD with reverential awe
and rejoice with trembling.
[12] Pay homage to the Son or he will be angry
and you will perish in your rebellion,
for his anger may ignite at any moment.
All who take refuge in him are happy.

King Amaziah Turns from the Lord

2 CHRONICLES 25

Judah's King Amaziah

[1] Amaziah became king when he was twenty-five years old, and he reigned twenty-nine years in Jerusalem. His mother's name was Jehoaddan; she was from Jerusalem. [2] He did what was right in the LORD's sight but not wholeheartedly.

[3] As soon as the kingdom was firmly in his grasp, he executed his servants who had killed his father the king. [4] However, he did not put their children to death, because—as it is written in the Law, in the book of Moses, where the LORD commanded—"Fathers are not to die because of children, and children are not to die because of fathers, but each one will die for his own sin."

Amaziah's Campaign Against Edom

[5] Then Amaziah gathered Judah and assembled them according to ancestral families, according to commanders of thousands, and according to commanders of hundreds. He numbered those twenty years old or more for all Judah and

Benjamin. He found there to be three hundred thousand fit young men who could serve in the army, bearing spear and shield. [6] Then for 7,500 pounds of silver he hired one hundred thousand valiant warriors from Israel.

[7] However, a man of God came to him and said, "King, do not let Israel's army go with you, for the LORD is not with Israel—all the Ephraimites. [8] But if you go with them, do it! Be strong for battle! But God will make you stumble before the enemy, for God has the power to help or to make one stumble."

[9] Then Amaziah said to the man of God, "What should I do about the 7,500 pounds of silver I gave to Israel's division?"

The man of God replied, "The LORD is able to give you much more than this."

[10] So Amaziah released the division that came to him from Ephraim to go home. But they got very angry with Judah and returned home in a fierce rage.

[11] Amaziah strengthened his position and led his people to the Salt Valley. He struck down ten thousand Seirites, [12] and the Judahites captured ten thousand alive. They took them to the top of a cliff where they threw them off, and all of them were dashed to pieces.

[13] As for the men of the division that Amaziah sent back so they would not go with him into battle, they raided the cities of Judah from Samaria to Beth-horon, struck down three thousand of their people, and took a great deal of plunder.

[14] After Amaziah came from the attack on the Edomites, he brought the gods of the Seirites and set them up as his gods. He worshiped before them and burned incense to them. [15] So the LORD's anger was against Amaziah, and he sent a prophet to him, who said, "Why have you sought a people's gods that could not rescue their own people from you?"

[16] While he was still speaking to him, the king asked, "Have we made you the king's counselor? Stop, why should you lose your life?"

So the prophet stopped, but he said, "I know that God intends to destroy you, because you have done this and have not listened to my advice."

Amaziah's War with Israel's King Jehoash

¹⁷ King Amaziah of Judah took counsel and sent word to Jehoash son of Jehoahaz, son of Jehu, king of Israel, and challenged him: "Come, let's meet face to face."

¹⁸ King Jehoash of Israel sent word to King Amaziah of Judah, saying, "The thistle in Lebanon sent a message to the cedar in Lebanon, saying, 'Give your daughter to my son as a wife.' Then a wild animal in Lebanon passed by and trampled the thistle. ¹⁹ You have said, 'Look, I have defeated Edom,' and you have become overconfident that you will get glory. Now stay at home. Why stir up such trouble so that you fall and Judah with you?"

²⁰ But Amaziah would not listen, for this turn of events was from God in order to hand them over to their enemies because they went after the gods of Edom. ²¹ So King Jehoash of Israel advanced. He and King Amaziah of Judah met face to face at Beth-shemesh that belonged to Judah. ²² Judah was routed before Israel, and each man fled to his own tent. ²³ King Jehoash of Israel captured Judah's King Amaziah son of Joash, son of Jehoahaz, at Beth-shemesh. Then Jehoash took him to Jerusalem and broke down two hundred yards of Jerusalem's wall from the Ephraim Gate to the Corner Gate. ²⁴ He took all the gold, silver, all the utensils that were found with Obed-edom in God's temple, the treasures of the king's palace, and the hostages. Then he returned to Samaria.

Amaziah's Death

²⁵ Judah's King Amaziah son of Joash lived fifteen years after the death of Israel's King Jehoash son of Jehoahaz. ²⁶ The rest of the events of Amaziah's reign, from beginning to end, are written in the Book of the Kings of Judah and Israel.

²⁷ From the time Amaziah turned from following the LORD, a conspiracy was formed against him in Jerusalem,

and he fled to Lachish. However, men were sent after him to Lachish, and they put him to death there. ²⁸ They carried him back on horses and buried him with his ancestors in the city of Judah.

2 CHRONICLES 26

Judah's King Uzziah

¹ All the people of Judah took Uzziah, who was sixteen years old, and made him king in place of his father Amaziah. ² After Amaziah the king rested with his ancestors, Uzziah rebuilt Eloth and restored it to Judah.

³ Uzziah was sixteen years old when he became king, and he reigned fifty-two years in Jerusalem. His mother's name was Jecoliah; she was from Jerusalem. ⁴ He did what was right in the LORD's sight just as his father Amaziah had done. ⁵ He sought God throughout the lifetime of Zechariah, the teacher of the fear of God. During the time that he sought the LORD, God gave him success.

Uzziah's Exploits

⁶ Uzziah went out to wage war against the Philistines, and he tore down the wall of Gath, the wall of Jabneh, and the wall of Ashdod. Then he built cities in the vicinity of Ashdod and among the Philistines. ⁷ God helped him against the Philistines, the Arabs that live in Gur-baal, and the Meunites. ⁸ The Ammonites paid tribute to Uzziah, and his fame spread as far as the entrance of Egypt, for God made him very powerful. ⁹ Uzziah built towers in Jerusalem at the Corner Gate, the Valley Gate, and the corner buttress, and he fortified them. ¹⁰ Since he had many cattle both in the Judean foothills and the plain, he built towers in the desert and dug many wells. And since he was a lover of the soil, he had farmers and vinedressers in the hills and in the fertile lands.

¹¹ Uzziah had an army equipped for combat that went out to war by division according to their assignments, as recorded by Jeiel the court secretary and Maaseiah the officer under the authority of Hananiah, one of the king's commanders. ¹² The total number of family heads was 2,600 valiant

warriors. [13] Under their authority was an army of 307,500 equipped for combat, a powerful force to help the king against the enemy. [14] Uzziah provided the entire army with shields, spears, helmets, armor, bows, and slingstones. [15] He made skillfully designed devices in Jerusalem to shoot arrows and catapult large stones for use on the towers and on the corners. So his fame spread even to distant places, for he was wondrously helped until he became strong.

Uzziah's Disease

[16] But when he became strong, he grew arrogant, and it led to his own destruction. He acted unfaithfully against the LORD his God by going into the LORD's sanctuary to burn incense on the incense altar. [17] The priest Azariah, along with eighty brave priests of the LORD, went in after him. [18] They took their stand against King Uzziah and said, "Uzziah, you have no right to offer incense to the LORD—only the consecrated priests, the descendants of Aaron, have the right to offer incense. Leave the sanctuary, for you have acted unfaithfully! You will not receive honor from the LORD God."

[19] Uzziah, with a firepan in his hand to offer incense, was enraged. But when he became enraged with the priests, in the presence of the priests in the LORD's temple beside the altar of incense, a skin disease broke out on his forehead. [20] Then Azariah the chief priest and all the priests turned to him and saw that he was diseased on his forehead. They rushed him out of there. He himself also hurried to get out because the LORD had afflicted him. [21] So King Uzziah was diseased to the time of his death. He lived in quarantine with a serious skin disease and was excluded from access to the LORD's temple, while his son Jotham was over the king's household governing the people of the land.

[22] Now the prophet Isaiah son of Amoz wrote about the rest of the events of Uzziah's reign, from beginning to end. [23] Uzziah rested with his ancestors, and he was buried with his ancestors in the burial ground of the kings' cemetery, for they said, "He has a skin disease." His son Jotham became king in his place.

🛡 GOING DEEPER

PROVERBS 16:18

Pride comes before destruction,
and an arrogant spirit before a fall.

Come, Thou Fount of Every Blessing

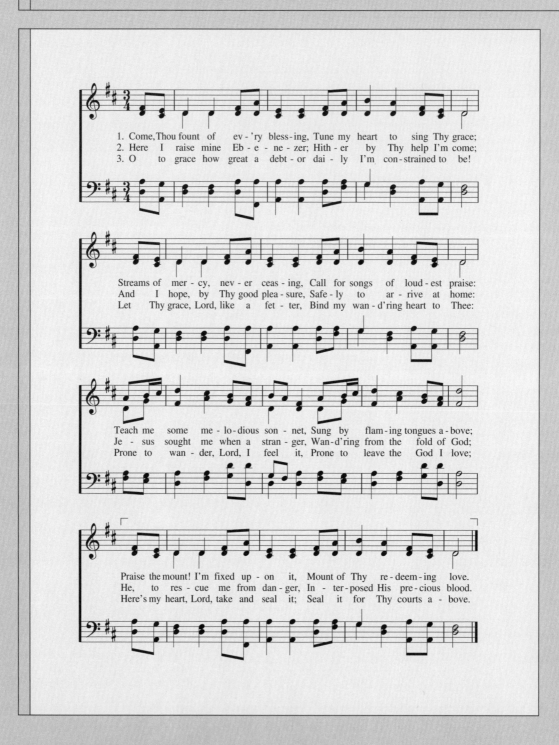

1. Come, Thou fount of ev-'ry bless-ing, Tune my heart to sing Thy grace;
2. Here I raise mine Eb-e-ne-zer; Hith-er by Thy help I'm come;
3. O to grace how great a debt-or dai-ly I'm con-strained to be!

Streams of mer-cy, nev-er ceas-ing, Call for songs of loud-est praise:
And I hope, by Thy good plea-sure, Safe-ly to ar-rive at home:
Let Thy grace, Lord, like a fet-ter, Bind my wan-d'ring heart to Thee:

Teach me some me-lo-dious son-net, Sung by flam-ing tongues a-bove;
Je-sus sought me when a stran-ger, Wan-d'ring from the fold of God;
Prone to wan-der, Lord, I feel it, Prone to leave the God I love;

Praise the mount! I'm fixed up-on it, Mount of Thy re-deem-ing love.
He, to res-cue me from dan-ger, In-ter-posed His pre-cious blood.
Here's my heart, Lord, take and seal it; Seal it for Thy courts a-bove.

WORDS: Robert Robinson

MUSIC: Traditional American melody; John Wyeth's *Repository of Sacred Music*; last stanza setting and choral ending by Billy Payne

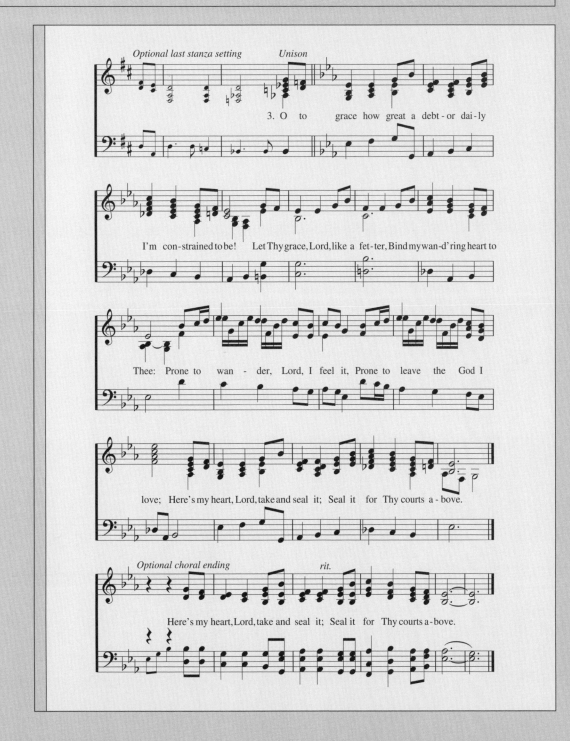

Grace Day

May your faithful love rest on us, LORD, for we put our hope in you.

PSALM 33:22

Take this day to catch up on your reading, pray, and rest in the presence of the Lord.

Weekly
Truth

Scripture is God-breathed and true. When we memorize it, we carry His Word with us wherever we go.

Over the last several weeks, we have memorized 1 Chronicles 29:11–13. Spend some time reviewing each of the verses as you commit the full passage to memory. Let David's prayer and praise inform your own.

See tips for memorizing Scripture on page 240.

Yours, LORD, is the greatness and the power and the glory and the splendor and the majesty, for everything in the heavens and on earth belongs to you. Yours, LORD, is the kingdom, and you are exalted as head over all. Riches and honor come from you, and you are the ruler of everything. Power and might are in your hand, and it is in your hand to make great and to give strength to all. Now therefore, our God, we give you thanks and praise your glorious name.

1 CHRONICLES 29:11-13

DAY 36

WEEK 6

King Ahaz's Unfaithfulness

2 CHRONICLES 27

Judah's King Jotham

¹ Jotham was twenty-five years old when he became king, and he reigned sixteen years in Jerusalem. His mother's name was Jerushah daughter of Zadok. ² He did what was right in the LORD's sight just as his father Uzziah had done. In addition, he didn't enter the LORD's sanctuary, but the people still behaved corruptly.

³ Jotham built the Upper Gate of the LORD's temple, and he built extensively on the wall of Ophel. ⁴ He also built cities in the hill country of Judah and fortresses and towers in the forests. ⁵ He waged war against the king of the Ammonites. He overpowered the Ammonites, and that year they gave him 7,500 pounds of silver, 60,000 bushels of wheat, and 60,000 bushels of barley. They paid him the same in the second and third years. ⁶ So Jotham strengthened his position because he did not waver in obeying the LORD his God.

⁷ As for the rest of the events of Jotham's reign, along with all his wars and his ways, note that they are written in the Book of the Kings of Israel and Judah. ⁸ He was twenty-five years old when he became king, and he reigned sixteen years in Jerusalem. ⁹ Jotham rested with his ancestors and was buried in the city of David. His son Ahaz became king in his place.

2 CHRONICLES 28

Judah's King Ahaz

¹ Ahaz was twenty years old when he became king, and he reigned sixteen years in Jerusalem. He did not do what was right in the LORD's sight like his ancestor David, ² for he walked in the ways of the kings of Israel and made cast images of the Baals. ³ He burned incense in Ben Hinnom Valley and burned his children in the fire, imitating the detestable practices of the nations the LORD had dispossessed before the Israelites. ⁴ He sacrificed and burned incense on the high places, on the hills, and under every green tree.

⁵ So the LORD his God handed Ahaz over to the king of Aram. He attacked him and took many captives to Damascus.

Ahaz was also handed over to the king of Israel, who struck him with great force: ⁶ Pekah son of Remaliah killed one hundred twenty thousand in Judah in one day—all brave men—because they had abandoned the LORD God of their ancestors. ⁷ An Ephraimite warrior named Zichri killed the king's son Maaseiah, Azrikam governor of the palace, and Elkanah who was second to the king. ⁸ Then the Israelites took two hundred thousand captives from their brothers—women, sons, and daughters. They also took a great deal of plunder from them and brought it to Samaria.

⁹ A prophet of the LORD named Oded was there. He went out to meet the army that came to Samaria and said to them, "Look, the LORD God of your ancestors handed them over to you because of his wrath against Judah, but you slaughtered them in a rage that has reached heaven.

¹⁰ Now you plan to reduce the people of Judah and Jerusalem, male and female, to slavery. Are you not also guilty before the LORD your God?

¹¹ Listen to me and return the captives you took from your brothers, for the Lᴏʀᴅ's burning anger is on you."

¹² So some men who were leaders of the Ephraimites—Azariah son of Jehohanan, Berechiah son of Meshillemoth, Jehizkiah son of Shallum, and Amasa son of Hadlai—stood in opposition to those coming from the war. ¹³ They said to them, "You must not bring the captives here, for you plan to bring guilt on us from the Lᴏʀᴅ to add to our sins and our guilt. For we have much guilt, and burning anger is on Israel."

¹⁴ The army left the captives and the plunder in the presence of the officers and the congregation. ¹⁵ Then the men who were designated by name took charge of the captives and provided clothes for their naked ones from the plunder. They clothed them, gave them sandals, food and drink, dressed their wounds, and provided donkeys for all the feeble. The Israelites brought them to Jericho, the City of Palms, among their brothers. Then they returned to Samaria.

¹⁶ At that time King Ahaz asked the king of Assyria for help. ¹⁷ The Edomites came again, attacked Judah, and took captives. ¹⁸ The Philistines also raided the cities of the Judean foothills and the Negev of Judah. They captured and occupied Beth-shemesh, Aijalon, and Gederoth, as well as Soco, Timnah, and Gimzo with their surrounding villages. ¹⁹ For the Lᴏʀᴅ humbled Judah because of King Ahaz of Judah, who threw off restraint in Judah and was unfaithful to the Lᴏʀᴅ. ²⁰ Then King Tiglath-pileser of Assyria came against Ahaz; he oppressed him and did not give him support. ²¹ Although Ahaz plundered the Lᴏʀᴅ's temple and the palace of the king and of the rulers and gave the plunder to the king of Assyria, it did not help him.

²² At the time of his distress, King Ahaz himself became more unfaithful to the Lᴏʀᴅ. ²³ He sacrificed to the gods of Damascus which had defeated him; he said, "Since the gods of the kings of Aram are helping them, I will sacrifice to them so that they will help me." But they were the downfall of him and of all Israel.

²⁴ Then Ahaz gathered up the utensils of God's temple, cut them into pieces, shut the doors of the Lᴏʀᴅ's temple, and made himself altars on every street corner in Jerusalem.

²⁵ He made high places in every city of Judah to offer incense to other gods, and he angered the Lᴏʀᴅ, the God of his ancestors.

Ahaz's Death

²⁶ As for the rest of his deeds and all his ways, from beginning to end, they are written in the Book of the Kings of Judah and Israel. ²⁷ Ahaz rested with his ancestors and was buried in the city, in Jerusalem, but they did not bring him into the tombs of the kings of Israel. His son Hezekiah became king in his place.

GOING DEEPER

DEUTERONOMY 27:15

"The person who makes a carved idol or cast image, which is detestable to
   the Lord, the work of a craftsman, and sets it up in secret is cursed."
And all the people will reply, "Amen!"

1 CORINTHIANS 10:14

So then, my dear friends, flee from idolatry.

NOTES

Renewal Under King Hezekiah

2 CHRONICLES 29

Judah's King Hezekiah

¹ Hezekiah was twenty-five years old when he became king, and he reigned twenty-nine years in Jerusalem. His mother's name was Abijah daughter of Zechariah. ² He did what was right in the LORD's sight just as his ancestor David had done.

³ In the first year of his reign, in the first month, he opened the doors of the LORD's temple and repaired them. ⁴ Then he brought in the priests and Levites and gathered them in the eastern public square. ⁵ He said to them, "Hear me, Levites. Consecrate yourselves now and consecrate the temple of the LORD, the God of your ancestors. Remove everything impure from the holy place. ⁶ For our ancestors were unfaithful and did what is evil in the sight of the LORD our God. They abandoned him, turned their faces away from the LORD's dwelling place, and turned their backs on him. ⁷ They also closed the doors of the portico, extinguished the lamps, did not burn incense, and did not offer burnt offerings in the holy place of the God of Israel. ⁸ Therefore, the wrath of the

LORD was on Judah and Jerusalem, and he made them an object of terror, horror, and mockery, as you see with your own eyes. ⁹ Our fathers fell by the sword, and our sons, our daughters, and our wives are in captivity because of this. ¹⁰ It is in my heart now to make a covenant with the LORD, the God of Israel so that his burning anger may turn away from us. ¹¹ My sons, don't be negligent now, for the LORD has chosen you to stand in his presence, to serve him, and to be his ministers and burners of incense."

Cleansing the Temple

¹² Then the Levites stood up:

Mahath son of Amasai and Joel son of Azariah from
    the Kohathites;
Kish son of Abdi and Azariah son of Jehallelel from
    the Merarites;
Joah son of Zimmah and Eden son of Joah from
    the Gershonites;
¹³ Shimri and Jeuel from the Elizaphanites;
Zechariah and Mattaniah from the Asaphites;
¹⁴ Jehiel and Shimei from the Hemanites;
Shemaiah and Uzziel from the Jeduthunites.

¹⁵ They gathered their brothers together, consecrated themselves, and went according to the king's command by the words of the LORD to cleanse the LORD's temple.

¹⁶ The priests went to the entrance of the LORD's temple to cleanse it. They took all the unclean things they found in the LORD's sanctuary to the courtyard of the LORD's temple. Then the Levites received them and took them outside to the Kidron Valley. ¹⁷ They began the consecration on the first day of the first month, and on the eighth day of the month they came to the portico of the LORD's temple.

They consecrated the LORD's temple for eight days, and on the sixteenth day of the first month they finished.

¹⁸ Then they went inside to King Hezekiah and said, "We have cleansed the whole temple of the LORD, the altar of burnt offering and all its utensils, and the table for the rows of the Bread of the Presence and all its utensils. ¹⁹ We have set up and consecrated all the utensils that King Ahaz rejected during his reign when he became unfaithful. They are in front of the altar of the LORD."

Renewal of Temple Worship

²⁰ King Hezekiah got up early, gathered the city officials, and went to the LORD's temple. ²¹ They brought seven bulls, seven rams, seven lambs, and seven male goats as a sin offering for the kingdom, for the sanctuary, and for Judah. Then he told the descendants of Aaron, the priests, to offer them on the altar of the LORD. ²² So they slaughtered the bulls, and the priests received the blood and splattered it on the altar. They slaughtered the rams and splattered the blood on the altar. They slaughtered the lambs and splattered the blood on the altar. ²³ Then they brought the goats for the sin offering right into the presence of the king and the congregation, who laid their hands on them. ²⁴ The priests slaughtered the goats and put their blood on the altar for a sin offering, to make atonement for all Israel, for the king said that the burnt offering and sin offering were for all Israel.

²⁵ Hezekiah stationed the Levites in the LORD's temple with cymbals, harps, and lyres according to the command of David, Gad the king's seer, and the prophet Nathan. For the command was from the LORD through his prophets. ²⁶ The Levites stood with the instruments of David, and the priests with the trumpets.

²⁷ Then Hezekiah ordered that the burnt offering be offered on the altar. When the burnt offerings began, the song of the LORD and the trumpets began, accompanied by the instruments of King David of Israel. ²⁸ The whole assembly was worshiping, singing the song, and blowing the trumpets—all this continued until the burnt offering was completed. ²⁹ When the burnt offerings were completed, the king and all those present with him bowed down and worshiped. ³⁰ Then King Hezekiah and the officials told the Levites to sing praise to the LORD in the words of David and of the seer Asaph. So they sang praises with rejoicing and knelt low and worshiped.

³¹ Hezekiah concluded, "Now you are consecrated to the LORD. Come near and bring sacrifices and thanksgiving offerings to the LORD's temple." So the congregation brought

sacrifices and thanksgiving offerings, and all those with willing hearts brought burnt offerings. 32 The number of burnt offerings the congregation brought was seventy bulls, one hundred rams, and two hundred lambs; all these were for a burnt offering to the LORD. 33 Six hundred bulls and three thousand sheep and goats were consecrated.

34 However, since there were not enough priests, they weren't able to skin all the burnt offerings, so their Levite brothers helped them until the work was finished and until the priests consecrated themselves. For the Levites were more conscientious to consecrate themselves than the priests were. 35 Furthermore, the burnt offerings were abundant, along with the fat of the fellowship offerings and with the drink offerings for the burnt offering.

So the service of the LORD's temple was established. 36 Then Hezekiah and all the people rejoiced over how God had prepared the people, for it had come about suddenly.

2 CHRONICLES 30

Celebration of the Passover

1 Then Hezekiah sent word throughout all Israel and Judah, and he also wrote letters to Ephraim and Manasseh to come to the LORD's temple in Jerusalem to observe the Passover of the LORD, the God of Israel. 2 For the king and his officials and the entire congregation in Jerusalem decided to observe the Passover of the LORD in the second month, 3 because they were not able to observe it at the appropriate time. Not enough of the priests had consecrated themselves, and the people hadn't been gathered together in Jerusalem. 4 The proposal pleased the king and the congregation, 5 so they affirmed the proposal and spread the message throughout all Israel, from Beer-sheba to Dan, to come to observe the Passover of the LORD, the God of Israel in Jerusalem, for they hadn't observed it often, as prescribed.

6 So the couriers went throughout Israel and Judah with letters from the hand of the king and his officials, and according to the king's command, saying, "Israelites, return to the LORD, the God of Abraham, Isaac, and Israel so that he may return to those of you who remain, who have escaped the grasp of the kings of Assyria. 7 Don't be like your ancestors and

your brothers who were unfaithful to the LORD, the God of their ancestors so that he made them an object of horror as you yourselves see. 8 Don't become obstinate now like your ancestors did. Give your allegiance to the LORD, and come to his sanctuary that he has consecrated forever. Serve the LORD your God so that he may turn his burning anger away from you, 9 for when you return to the LORD, your brothers and your sons will receive mercy in the presence of their captors and will return to this land. For the LORD your God is gracious and merciful; he will not turn his face away from you if you return to him."

10 The couriers traveled from city to city in the land of Ephraim and Manasseh as far as Zebulun, but the inhabitants laughed at them and mocked them. 11 But some from Asher, Manasseh, and Zebulun humbled themselves and came to Jerusalem. 12 Also, the power of God was at work in Judah to unite them to carry out the command of the king and his officials by the word of the LORD.

13 A very large assembly of people was gathered in Jerusalem to observe the Festival of Unleavened Bread in the second month. 14 They proceeded to take away the altars that were in Jerusalem, and they took away the incense altars and threw them into the Kidron Valley. 15 They slaughtered the Passover lamb on the fourteenth day of the second month. The priests and Levites were ashamed, and they consecrated themselves and brought burnt offerings to the LORD's temple. 16 They stood at their prescribed posts, according to the law of Moses, the man of God. The priests splattered the blood received from the Levites, 17 for there were many in the assembly who had not consecrated themselves, and so the Levites were in charge of slaughtering the Passover lambs for every unclean person to consecrate the lambs to the LORD. 18 A large number of the people—many from Ephraim, Manasseh, Issachar, and Zebulun—were ritually unclean, yet they had eaten the Passover contrary to what was written. But Hezekiah had interceded for them, saying, "May the good Lord provide atonement on behalf of 19 whoever sets his whole heart on seeking God, the LORD, the God of his ancestors, even though not according to the purification rules of the sanctuary." 20 So the LORD heard Hezekiah and healed the people. 21 The Israelites who were present in Jerusalem observed the Festival of Unleavened

Bread seven days with great joy, and the Levites and the priests praised the LORD day after day with loud instruments. ²² Then Hezekiah encouraged all the Levites who performed skillfully before the LORD. They ate at the appointed festival for seven days, sacrificing fellowship offerings and giving thanks to the LORD, the God of their ancestors.

²³ The whole congregation decided to observe seven more days, so they observed seven days with joy, ²⁴ for King Hezekiah of Judah contributed one thousand bulls and seven thousand sheep for the congregation. Also, the officials contributed one thousand bulls and ten thousand sheep for the congregation, and many priests consecrated themselves. ²⁵ Then the whole assembly of Judah with the priests and Levites, the whole assembly that came from Israel, the resident aliens who came from the land of Israel, and those who were living in Judah, rejoiced. ²⁶ There was great rejoicing in Jerusalem, for nothing like this was known since the days of Solomon son of David, the king of Israel.

²⁷ Then the priests and the Levites stood to bless the people,

and God heard them, and their prayer came into his holy dwelling place in heaven.

2 CHRONICLES 31

Removal of Idolatry

¹ When all this was completed, all Israel who had attended went out to the cities of Judah and broke up the sacred pillars, chopped down the Asherah poles, and tore down the high places and altars throughout Judah and Benjamin, as well as in Ephraim and Manasseh, to the last one. Then all the Israelites returned to their cities, each to his own possession.

Offerings for Levites

² Hezekiah reestablished the divisions of the priests and Levites for the burnt offerings and fellowship offerings, for ministry, for giving thanks, and for praise in the gates of the camp of the LORD, each division corresponding to his service among the priests and Levites. ³ The king contributed from his own possessions for the regular morning and evening burnt offerings, the burnt offerings of the Sabbaths, of the New Moons, and of the appointed feasts, as written in the law of the LORD. ⁴ He told the people who lived in Jerusalem to give a contribution for the priests and Levites so that they could devote their energy to the law of the LORD. ⁵ When the word spread, the Israelites gave liberally of the best of the grain, new wine, fresh oil, honey, and of all the produce of the field, and they brought in an abundance, a tenth of everything. ⁶ As for the Israelites and Judahites who lived in the cities of Judah, they also brought a tenth of the herds and flocks, and a tenth of the dedicated things

that were consecrated to the LORD their God. They gathered them into large piles. [7] In the third month they began building up the piles, and they finished in the seventh month. [8] When Hezekiah and his officials came and viewed the piles, they blessed the LORD and his people Israel.

[9] Hezekiah asked the priests and Levites about the piles. [10] The chief priest Azariah, of the household of Zadok, answered him, "Since they began bringing the offering to the LORD's temple, we have been eating and are satisfied and there is plenty left over because the LORD has blessed his people; this abundance is what is left over."

[11] Hezekiah told them to prepare chambers in the LORD's temple, and they prepared them. [12] The offering, the tenth, and the dedicated things were brought faithfully. Conaniah the Levite was the officer in charge of them, and his brother Shimei was second. [13] Jehiel, Azaziah, Nahath, Asahel, Jerimoth, Jozabad, Eliel, Ismachiah, Mahath, and Benaiah were deputies under the authority of Conaniah and his brother Shimei by appointment of King Hezekiah and of Azariah the chief official of God's temple.

[14] Kore son of Imnah the Levite, the keeper of the East Gate, was over the freewill offerings to God to distribute the contribution to the LORD and the consecrated things. [15] Eden, Miniamin, Jeshua, Shemaiah, Amariah, and Shecaniah in the cities of the priests were to distribute it faithfully under his authority to their brothers by divisions, whether large or small. [16] In addition, they distributed it to males registered by genealogy three years old and above; to all who would enter the LORD's temple for their daily duty, for their service in their responsibilities according to their divisions. [17] They distributed also to those recorded by genealogy of the priests by their ancestral families and the Levites twenty years old and above, by their responsibilities in their divisions; [18] to those registered by genealogy—with all their dependents, wives, sons, and daughters—of the whole assembly (for they had faithfully consecrated themselves as holy); [19] and to the descendants of Aaron, the priests, in the common fields of their cities, in each and every city. There were men who were registered by name to distribute a portion to every male among the priests and to every Levite recorded by genealogy.

[20] Hezekiah did this throughout all Judah.

He did what was good and upright and true before the LORD his God. [21] He was diligent in every deed that he began in the service of God's temple, in the instruction and the commands, in order to seek his God, and he prospered.

MICAH 6:6-8

⁶ What should I bring before the LORD
when I come to bow before God on high?
Should I come before him with burnt offerings,
with year-old calves?
⁷ Would the LORD be pleased with thousands of rams
or with ten thousand streams of oil?
Should I give my firstborn for my transgression,
the offspring of my body for my own sin?

⁸ Mankind, he has told each of you what is good
and what it is the LORD requires of you:
to act justly,
to love faithfulness,
and to walk humbly with your God.

Christ as Prophet, Priest, and King

In 1 & 2 Chronicles, the author repeatedly uses covenant language to describe God's forever, faithful relationship with His people, along with its blessings and responsibilities. More than an agreement or list of rules, covenants were a means of defining Israel's relationship with God and teaching them about His character and salvation.

God established the three offices of prophet, priest, and king to lead His people. They not only helped to mediate Israel's relationship with God, but they also pointed to the hope of a new, eternal covenant that would be brought about by the Messiah. The New Testament writers celebrate Jesus Christ as this Messiah—the true Prophet, Priest, and King. He is the divine Son of God, the heir to David's throne, and the One who reigns forever and ever. During the season of Lent, we turn to Scripture to remember and rejoice that Jesus Christ took on each of these unique roles of authority and fulfilled them perfectly as no one else could.

A Prophet...

— Speaks on behalf of God to His people, reminding them of God's covenant blessings and their covenant responsibilities.

— Declares the truth of God's living Word.

— Proclaims God's coming judgment on His people, calling them to repent and turn away from sin.

— Inspires vision and hope for lasting restoration.

THEN

In the Old Testament, prophets were set apart to deliver God's Word. They proclaimed God's coming judgment, highlighting both the discipline and healing that would come to God's people who were in need of salvation. In Israel's recorded history in Chronicles, the nation constantly needed to be reminded of their covenant relationship. The prophets' messages concerned both the present and the future. For example, the prophet Nathan interacted with King David on several occasions, communicating God's instructions regarding various circumstances (1Ch 17:1–15).

NOW

Long ago God spoke to our ancestors by the prophets at different times and in different ways. In these last days, he has spoken to us by his Son.

HEBREWS 1:1–2

Because Jesus Christ was both a messenger of redemption and the means through which it was accomplished, He is above all other prophets. Jesus is still our perfect Prophet. He calls us to share in the work of proclaiming a message of salvation and mercy secured through His life, death, and resurrection.

REFERENCES: MT 5:17; 16:15–16

Continued

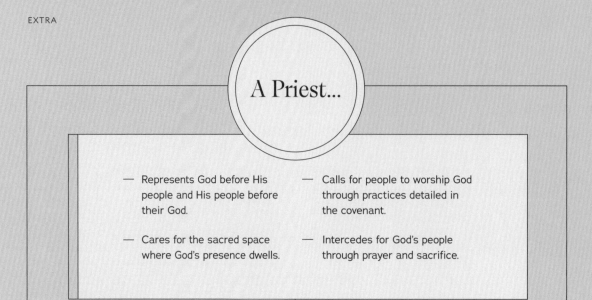

A Priest...

— Represents God before His people and His people before their God.

— Cares for the sacred space where God's presence dwells.

— Calls for people to worship God through practices detailed in the covenant.

— Intercedes for God's people through prayer and sacrifice.

THEN

In the Old Testament, priests tended to the tabernacle where the presence of God dwelled. The priests worked to anchor God's people in the practice of worship. They brought imperfect sacrifices for imperfect people before a holy God, asking Him to forgive them. Chronicles details the priestly lineage and the divisions of responsibilities under David's and Solomon's reigns (1Ch 6). The priestly responsibilities established by God through Moses are restated, reminding the people of how worship must remain central to their identity as God's covenant people.

NOW

Therefore, since we have a great high priest who has passed through the heavens—Jesus the Son of God—let us hold fast to our confession.

HEBREWS 4:14

Christ is our perfect High Priest. He brought us peace with God by offering Himself up as the perfect, substitutionary sacrifice and asks us to share in the work of interceding for others.

REFERENCES: JN 17:1–26; 1TM 2:5; HEB 4:14–16; 9:11–15

A King...

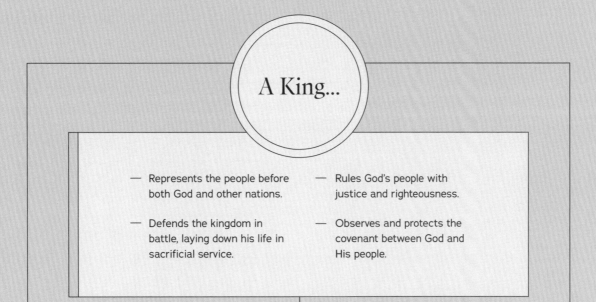

— Represents the people before both God and other nations.

— Defends the kingdom in battle, laying down his life in sacrificial service.

— Rules God's people with justice and righteousness.

— Observes and protects the covenant between God and His people.

THEN

In the Old Testament, kings had the choice to either follow God's commands and covenants, which led to His blessing, or reject Him and suffer the consequences along with their people. In 1 Chronicles, King David expresses his desire to make a permanent house for God in Jerusalem. God responded by saying He would make a house for David—a royal line that would never come to an end (1Ch 17:10–14). Each subsequent king was called to follow after David by keeping the statutes and commands of God. Though the monarchy came to an end when the people of Judah were taken into exile by the Babylonians, God's promise remained. During the Babylonian exile, the prophets continued to speak of a coming Messiah, an "anointed one" from the line of David who would reign as a righteous King without end (Is 9:6–7).

NOW

...at the name of Jesus every knee will bow—in heaven and on earth and under the earth—and every tongue will confess that Jesus Christ is Lord, to the glory of God the Father.

PHILIPPIANS 2:10–11

Although Jesus came to earth in the humblest way imaginable, He was born King of the Jews, or more specifically, King of the people of God. All authority in heaven and on earth has been given to Him, and He conquers the enemy, protects us, and shapes us into God's people. Christ is the perfect King. He calls us to share in His holy work of defending and serving others who bear the image of God.

REFERENCES: IS 9:7; MT 28:18; 2TH 3:3; HEB 6:10; RV 19:16

Manasseh's
Repentance

2 CHRONICLES 32

Sennacherib's Invasion

¹ After Hezekiah's faithful deeds, King Sennacherib of Assyria came and entered Judah. He laid siege to the fortified cities and intended to break into them. ² Hezekiah saw that Sennacherib had come and that he planned war on Jerusalem, ³ so he consulted with his officials and his warriors about stopping up the water of the springs that were outside the city, and they helped him. ⁴ Many people gathered and stopped up all the springs and the stream that flowed through the land; they said, "Why should the kings of Assyria come and find abundant water?" ⁵ Then Hezekiah strengthened his position by rebuilding the entire broken-down wall and heightening the towers and the other outside wall. He repaired the supporting terraces of the city of David, and made an abundance of weapons and shields.

⁶ He set military commanders over the people and gathered the people in the square of the city gate. Then he encouraged them, saying, ⁷ "Be strong and courageous! Don't be afraid or discouraged before the king of Assyria or before the large army that is with him, for there are more with us than with him. ⁸ He has only human strength, but we have the LORD our God to help us and to fight our battles." So the people relied on the words of King Hezekiah of Judah.

Sennacherib's Servant's Speech

⁹ After this, while King Sennacherib of Assyria with all his armed forces besieged Lachish, he sent his servants to Jerusalem against King Hezekiah of Judah and against all those of Judah who were in Jerusalem, saying, ¹⁰ "This is what King Sennacherib of Assyria says: 'What are you relying on that you remain in Jerusalem under siege? ¹¹ Isn't Hezekiah misleading you to give you over to death by famine and thirst when he says, "The LORD our God will keep us from the grasp of the king of Assyria"? ¹² Didn't Hezekiah himself remove his high places and his altars and say to Judah and Jerusalem, "You must worship before one altar, and you must burn incense on it"?

¹³ "'Don't you know what I and my predecessors have done to all the peoples of the lands? Have any of the national gods of the lands been able to rescue their land from my power? ¹⁴ Who among all the gods of these nations that my

predecessors completely destroyed was able to rescue his people from my power, that your God should be able to deliver you from my power? [15] So now, don't let Hezekiah deceive you, and don't let him mislead you like this. Don't believe him, for no god of any nation or kingdom has been able to rescue his people from my power or the power of my predecessors. How much less will your God rescue you from my power!'"

[16] His servants said more against the LORD God and against his servant Hezekiah. [17] He also wrote letters to mock the LORD, the God of Israel, saying against him:

Just like the national gods of the lands that did not rescue their people from my power, so Hezekiah's God will not rescue his people from my power.

[18] Then they called out loudly in Hebrew to the people of Jerusalem, who were on the wall, to frighten and discourage them in order that he might capture the city. [19] They spoke against the God of Jerusalem like they had spoken against the gods of the peoples of the earth, which were made by human hands.

Deliverance from Sennacherib

[20] King Hezekiah and the prophet Isaiah son of Amoz prayed about this and cried out to heaven, [21] and the LORD sent an angel who annihilated every valiant warrior, leader, and commander in the camp of the king of Assyria. So the king of Assyria returned in disgrace to his land. He went to the temple of his god, and there some of his own children struck him down with the sword.

[22] So the LORD saved Hezekiah and the inhabitants of Jerusalem from the power of King Sennacherib of Assyria and from the power of all others. He gave them rest on every side. [23] Many were bringing an offering to the LORD to Jerusalem and valuable gifts to King Hezekiah of Judah, and he was exalted in the eyes of all the nations after that.

Hezekiah's Illness and Pride

[24] In those days Hezekiah became sick to the point of death, so he prayed to the LORD, who spoke to him and gave him a miraculous sign. [25] However, because his heart was proud, Hezekiah didn't respond according to the benefit that had come to him. So there was wrath on him, Judah, and Jerusalem. [26] Then Hezekiah humbled himself for the pride of his heart—he and the inhabitants of Jerusalem—so the LORD's wrath didn't come on them during Hezekiah's lifetime.

Hezekiah's Wealth and Works

[27] Hezekiah had abundant riches and glory, and he made himself treasuries for silver, gold, precious stones, spices, shields, and every desirable item. [28] He made

warehouses for the harvest of grain, new wine, and fresh oil, and stalls for all kinds of cattle, and pens for flocks. ²⁹ He made cities for himself, and he acquired vast numbers of flocks and herds, for God gave him abundant possessions.

³⁰ This same Hezekiah blocked the upper outlet of the water from the Gihon Spring and channeled it smoothly downward and westward to the city of David. Hezekiah succeeded in everything he did. ³¹ When the ambassadors of Babylon's rulers were sent to him to inquire about the miraculous sign that happened in the land, God left him to test him and discover what was in his heart.

Hezekiah's Death

³² As for the rest of the events of Hezekiah's reign and his deeds of faithful love, note that they are written in the Visions of the Prophet Isaiah son of Amoz, and in the Book of the Kings of Judah and Israel. ³³ Hezekiah rested with his ancestors and was buried on the ascent to the tombs of David's descendants. All Judah and the inhabitants of Jerusalem paid him honor at his death. His son Manasseh became king in his place.

2 CHRONICLES 33

Judah's King Manasseh

¹ Manasseh was twelve years old when he became king, and he reigned fifty-five years in Jerusalem. ² He did what was evil in the LORD's sight, imitating the detestable practices of the nations that the LORD had dispossessed before the Israelites. ³ He rebuilt the high places that his father Hezekiah had torn down and reestablished the altars for the Baals. He made Asherah poles, and he bowed in worship to all the stars in the sky and served them. ⁴ He built altars in the LORD's temple, where the LORD had said, "Jerusalem is where my name will remain forever." ⁵ He built altars to all the stars in the sky in both courtyards of the LORD's temple. ⁶ He passed his sons through the fire in Ben Hinnom Valley. He practiced witchcraft, divination, and sorcery, and consulted mediums and spiritists. He did a huge amount of evil in the LORD's sight, angering him.

⁷ Manasseh set up a carved image of the idol, which he had made, in God's temple that God had spoken about to David and his son Solomon: "I will establish my name forever in this temple and in Jerusalem, which I have chosen out of all the tribes of Israel. ⁸ I will never again remove the feet of the Israelites from the land where I stationed your ancestors, if only they will be careful to do all I have commanded them through Moses—all the law, statutes, and judgments." ⁹ So Manasseh caused Judah and the inhabitants of Jerusalem to stray so that they did worse evil than the nations the LORD had destroyed before the Israelites.

Manasseh's Repentance

[10] The LORD spoke to Manasseh and his people, but they didn't listen. [11] So he brought against them the military commanders of the king of Assyria. They captured Manasseh with hooks, bound him with bronze shackles, and took him to Babylon. [12] When he was in distress, he sought the favor of the LORD his God and earnestly humbled himself before the God of his ancestors. [13] He prayed to him, and the LORD was receptive to his prayer. He granted his request and brought him back to Jerusalem, to his kingdom. So Manasseh came to know that the LORD is God.

[14] After this, he built the outer wall of the city of David from west of Gihon in the valley to the entrance of the Fish Gate; he brought it around Ophel, and he heightened it considerably. He also placed military commanders in all the fortified cities of Judah.

[15] He removed the foreign gods and the idol from the LORD's temple, along with all the altars that he had built on the mountain of the LORD's temple and in Jerusalem, and he threw them outside the city.

[16] He built the altar of the LORD and offered fellowship and thanksgiving sacrifices on it. Then he told Judah to serve the LORD, the God of Israel. [17] However, the people still sacrificed at the high places, but only to the LORD their God.

Manasseh's Death

[18] The rest of the events of Manasseh's reign, along with his prayer to his God and the words of the seers who spoke to him in the name of the LORD, the God of Israel, are written in the Events of Israel's Kings. [19] His prayer and how God was receptive to his prayer, and all his sin and unfaithfulness and the sites where he built high places and set up Asherah poles and carved images before he humbled himself, they are written in the Events of Hozai. [20] Manasseh rested with his ancestors, and he was buried in his own house. His son Amon became king in his place.

Judah's King Amon

[21] Amon was twenty-two years old when he became king, and he reigned two years in Jerusalem. [22] He did what was evil in the LORD's sight, just as his father Manasseh had done. Amon sacrificed to all the carved images that his father Manasseh had made, and he served them. [23] But he did not humble himself before the LORD like his father Manasseh humbled himself; instead, Amon increased his guilt.

[24] So his servants conspired against him and put him to death in his own house.

²⁵ The common people killed all who had conspired against King Amon, and they made his son Josiah king in his place.

◗ GOING DEEPER

1 TIMOTHY 1:15

This saying is trustworthy and deserving of full acceptance: "Christ Jesus came into the world to save sinners"—and I am the worst of them.

King Josiah Renews the Covenant

2 CHRONICLES 34

Judah's King Josiah

¹ Josiah was eight years old when he became king, and he reigned thirty-one years in Jerusalem. ² He did what was right in the Lord's sight and walked in the ways of his ancestor David; he did not turn aside to the right or the left.

Josiah's Reform

³ In the eighth year of his reign, while he was still a youth, Josiah began to seek the God of his ancestor David, and in the twelfth year he began to cleanse Judah and Jerusalem of the high places, the Asherah poles, the carved images, and the cast images. ⁴ Then in his presence the altars of the Baals were torn down, and he chopped down the shrines that were above them. He shattered the Asherah poles, the carved images, and the cast images, crushed them to dust, and scattered them over the graves of those who had sacrificed to them. ⁵ He burned the bones of the priests on their altars. So he cleansed Judah and Jerusalem. ⁶ He did the same in the cities of Manasseh, Ephraim, and Simeon, and as

far as Naphtali and on their surrounding mountain shrines. [7] He tore down the altars, and he smashed the Asherah poles and the carved images to powder. He chopped down all the shrines throughout the land of Israel and returned to Jerusalem.

Josiah's Repair of the Temple

[8] In the eighteenth year of his reign, in order to cleanse the land and the temple, Josiah sent Shaphan son of Azaliah, along with Maaseiah the governor of the city and the court historian Joah son of Joahaz, to repair the temple of the LORD his God.

[9] So they went to the high priest Hilkiah and gave him the silver brought into God's temple. The Levites and the doorkeepers had collected it from Manasseh, Ephraim, and from the entire remnant of Israel, and from all Judah, Benjamin, and the inhabitants of Jerusalem. [10] They gave it to those doing the work—those who oversaw the LORD's temple. They gave it to the workmen who were working in the LORD's temple, to repair and restore the temple; [11] they gave it to the carpenters and builders and also used it to buy quarried stone and timbers—for joining and making beams—for the buildings that Judah's kings had destroyed.

[12] The men were doing the work with integrity. Their overseers were Jahath and Obadiah, Levites from the Merarites, and Zechariah and Meshullam from the Kohathites as supervisors. The Levites were all skilled with musical instruments. [13] They were also over the porters and were supervising all those doing the work task by task. Some of the Levites were secretaries, officers, and gatekeepers.

The Recovery of the Book of the Law

[14] When they brought out the silver that had been deposited in the LORD's temple, the priest Hilkiah found the book of the law of the LORD written by the hand of Moses. [15] Consequently, Hilkiah told the court secretary Shaphan, "I have found the book of the law in the LORD's temple," and he gave the book to Shaphan.

¹⁶ Shaphan took the book to the king, and also reported, "Your servants are doing all that was placed in their hands. ¹⁷ They have emptied out the silver that was found in the Lord's temple and have given it to the overseers and to those doing the work." ¹⁸ Then the court secretary Shaphan told the king, "The priest Hilkiah gave me a book," and Shaphan read from it in the presence of the king.

¹⁹ When the king heard the words of the law, he tore his clothes. ²⁰ Then he commanded Hilkiah, Ahikam son of Shaphan, Abdon son of Micah, the court secretary Shaphan, and the king's servant Asaiah, ²¹ "Go and inquire of the Lord for me and for those remaining in Israel and Judah, concerning the words of the book that was found. For great is the Lord's wrath that is poured out on us because our ancestors have not kept the word of the Lord in order to do everything written in this book."

Huldah's Prophecy of Judgment

²² So Hilkiah and those the king had designated went to the prophetess Huldah, the wife of Shallum son of Tokhath, son of Hasrah, keeper of the wardrobe. She lived in Jerusalem in the Second District. They spoke with her about this.

²³ She said to them, "This is what the Lord God of Israel says: Say to the man who sent you to me, ²⁴ 'This is what the Lord says: I am about to bring disaster on this place and on its inhabitants, fulfilling all the curses written in the book that they read in the presence of the king of Judah, ²⁵ because they have abandoned me and burned incense to other gods so as to anger me with all the works of their hands. My wrath will be poured out on this place, and it will not be quenched.' ²⁶ Say this to the king of Judah who sent you to inquire of the Lord:

'This is what the Lord God of Israel says:
As for the words that you heard, ²⁷ because
your heart was tender and you humbled
yourself before God when you heard his words
against this place and against its inhabitants,
and because you humbled yourself before
me, and you tore your clothes and wept
before me, I myself have heard'

—this is the Lord's declaration. ²⁸ 'I will indeed gather you to your ancestors, and you will be gathered to your grave in peace. Your eyes will not see all the disaster that I am bringing on this place and on its inhabitants.'"

Then they reported to the king.

Affirmation of the Covenant by Josiah and the People

²⁹ So the king sent messengers and gathered all the elders of Judah and Jerusalem. ³⁰ The king went up to the LORD's temple with all the men of Judah and the inhabitants of Jerusalem, as well as the priests and the Levites—all the people from the oldest to the youngest. He read in their hearing all the words of the book of the covenant that had been found in the LORD's temple. ³¹ Then the king stood at his post and made a covenant in the LORD's presence to follow the LORD and to keep his commands, his decrees, and his statutes with all his heart and with all his soul in order to carry out the words of the covenant written in this book.

³² He had all those present in Jerusalem and Benjamin agree to it. So all the inhabitants of Jerusalem carried out the covenant of God, the God of their ancestors.

³³ So Josiah removed everything that was detestable from all the lands belonging to the Israelites, and he required all who were present in Israel to serve the LORD their God. Throughout his reign they did not turn aside from following the LORD, the God of their ancestors.

2 CHRONICLES 35

Josiah's Passover Observance

¹ Josiah observed the LORD's Passover and slaughtered the Passover lambs on the fourteenth day of the first month. ² He appointed the priests to their responsibilities and encouraged them to serve in the LORD's temple. ³ He said to the Levites who taught all Israel the holy things of the LORD, "Put the holy ark in the temple built by Solomon son of David king of Israel. Since you do not have to carry it on your shoulders, now serve the LORD your God and his people Israel.

⁴ "Organize your ancestral families by your divisions according to the written instruction of King David of Israel and that of his son Solomon. ⁵ Serve in the holy place by the groupings of the ancestral families for your brothers, the lay people, and according to the division of the Levites by family. ⁶ Slaughter the Passover lambs, consecrate yourselves, and make preparations for your brothers to carry out the word of the LORD through Moses."

⁷ Then Josiah donated thirty thousand sheep, lambs, and young goats, plus three thousand cattle from his own possessions, for the Passover sacrifices for all the lay people who were present.

⁸ His officials also donated willingly for the people, the priests, and the Levites. Hilkiah, Zechariah, and Jehiel, chief officials of God's temple, gave twenty-six

hundred Passover sacrifices and three hundred cattle for the priests. [9] Conaniah and his brothers Shemaiah and Nethanel, and Hashabiah, Jeiel, and Jozabad, officers of the Levites, donated five thousand Passover sacrifices for the Levites, plus five hundred cattle.

[10] So the service was established; the priests stood at their posts and the Levites in their divisions according to the king's command. [11] Then they slaughtered the Passover lambs, and while the Levites were skinning the animals, the priests splattered the blood they had been given. [12] They removed the burnt offerings so that they might be given to the groupings of the ancestral families of the lay people to offer to the LORD, according to what is written in the book of Moses; they did the same with the cattle. [13] They roasted the Passover lambs with fire according to regulation. They boiled the holy sacrifices in pots, kettles, and bowls; and they quickly brought them to the lay people. [14] Afterward, they made preparations for themselves and for the priests, since the priests, the descendants of Aaron, were busy offering up burnt offerings and fat until night. So the Levites made preparations for themselves and for the priests, the descendants of Aaron.

[15] The singers, the descendants of Asaph, were at their stations according to the command of David, Asaph, Heman, and Jeduthun the king's seer. Also, the gatekeepers were at each temple gate. None of them left their tasks because their Levite brothers had made preparations for them.

[16] So all the service of the LORD was established that day for observing the Passover and for offering burnt offerings on the altar of the LORD, according to the command of King Josiah. [17] The Israelites who were present in Judah also observed the Passover at that time and the Festival of Unleavened Bread for seven days. [18] No Passover had been observed like it in Israel since the days of the prophet Samuel. None of the kings of Israel ever observed a Passover like the one that Josiah observed with the priests, the Levites, all Judah, the Israelites who were present in Judah, and the inhabitants of Jerusalem. [19] In the eighteenth year of Josiah's reign, this Passover was observed.

Josiah's Last Deeds and Death

[20] After all this that Josiah had prepared for the temple, King Neco of Egypt marched up to fight at Carchemish by the Euphrates, and Josiah went out to confront him. [21] But Neco sent messengers to him, saying, "What is the issue between you and me, king of Judah? I have not come against you today but I am fighting another dynasty. God told me to hurry. Stop opposing God who is with me; don't make him destroy you!"

[22] But Josiah did not turn away from him; instead, in order to fight with him he disguised himself. He did not listen to Neco's words from the mouth of God, but went to the Valley of Megiddo to fight. [23] The archers shot King Josiah, and he said

to his servants, "Take me away, for I am severely wounded!" ²⁴ So his servants took him out of the war chariot, carried him in his second chariot, and brought him to Jerusalem. Then he died, and they buried him in the tomb of his ancestors. All Judah and Jerusalem mourned for Josiah. ²⁵ Jeremiah chanted a dirge over Josiah, and all the male and female singers still speak of Josiah in their dirges today. They established them as a statute for Israel, and indeed they are written in the Dirges.

²⁶ The rest of the events of Josiah's reign, along with his deeds of faithful love according to what is written in the law of the LORD, ²⁷ and his words, from beginning to end, are written in the Book of the Kings of Israel and Judah.

◖ GOING DEEPER

PSALM 1:1-3

The Two Ways

¹ How happy is the one who does not
walk in the advice of the wicked
or stand in the pathway with sinners
or sit in the company of mockers!
² Instead, his delight is in the LORD's instruction,
and he meditates on it day and night.
³ He is like a tree planted beside flowing streams
that bears its fruit in its season,
and its leaf does not wither.
Whatever he does prospers.

The Last Kings of Judah

2 CHRONICLES 36

Judah's King Jehoahaz

¹ Then the common people took Jehoahaz son of Josiah and made him king in Jerusalem in place of his father.

² Jehoahaz was twenty-three years old when he became king, and he reigned three months in Jerusalem. ³ The king of Egypt deposed him in Jerusalem and fined the land seventy-five hundred pounds of silver and seventy-five pounds of gold.

Judah's King Jehoiakim

⁴ Then King Neco of Egypt made Jehoahaz's brother Eliakim king over Judah and Jerusalem and changed Eliakim's name to Jehoiakim. But Neco took his brother Jehoahaz and brought him to Egypt.

⁵ Jehoiakim was twenty-five years old when he became king, and he reigned eleven years in Jerusalem. He did what was evil in the sight of the LORD his God. ⁶ Now King Nebuchadnezzar of Babylon attacked him and bound him in bronze shackles to take him to Babylon. ⁷ Also Nebuchadnezzar took some of the articles of the LORD's temple to Babylon and put them in his temple in Babylon.

⁸ The rest of the deeds of Jehoiakim, the detestable actions he committed, and what was found against him, are written in the Book of Israel's Kings. His son Jehoiachin became king in his place.

Judah's King Jehoiachin

⁹ Jehoiachin was eighteen years old when he became king, and he reigned three months and ten days in Jerusalem. He did what was evil in the LORD's sight. ¹⁰ In the spring Nebuchadnezzar sent for him and brought him to Babylon along with the valuable articles of the LORD's temple. Then he made Jehoiachin's brother Zedekiah king over Judah and Jerusalem.

Judah's King Zedekiah

¹¹ Zedekiah was twenty-one years old when he became king, and he reigned eleven years in Jerusalem. ¹² He did what was evil in the sight of the LORD his God and did not humble himself before the prophet Jeremiah at the LORD's command. ¹³ He also rebelled against King Nebuchadnezzar who had made him swear allegiance by God. He became obstinate and hardened his heart against returning to the LORD, the God of Israel. ¹⁴ All the leaders of the priests and the people multiplied their unfaithful deeds, imitating all the detestable practices of the nations, and they defiled the LORD's temple that he had consecrated in Jerusalem.

The Destruction of Jerusalem

¹⁵ But the LORD, the God of their ancestors sent word against them by the hand of his messengers, sending them time and time again, for he had compassion on his people and on his dwelling place.

¹⁶ But they kept ridiculing God's messengers, despising his words, and scoffing at his prophets, until the LORD's wrath

was so stirred up against his people that there was no remedy. [17] So he brought up against them the king of the Chaldeans, who killed their fit young men with the sword in the house of their sanctuary. He had no pity on young men or young women, elderly or aged; he handed them all over to him. [18] He took everything to Babylon—all the articles of God's temple, large and small, the treasures of the LORD's temple, and the treasures of the king and his officials. [19] Then the Chaldeans burned God's temple. They tore down Jerusalem's wall, burned all its palaces, and destroyed all its valuable articles.

[20] He deported those who escaped from the sword to Babylon, and they became servants to him and his sons until the rise of the Persian kingdom. [21] This fulfilled the word of the LORD through Jeremiah, and the land enjoyed its Sabbath rest all the days of the desolation until seventy years were fulfilled.

The Decree of Cyrus

[22] In the first year of King Cyrus of Persia, in order to fulfill the word of the LORD spoken through Jeremiah, the LORD roused the spirit of King Cyrus of Persia to issue a proclamation throughout his entire kingdom and also to put it in writing:

[23] This is what King Cyrus of Persia says: The LORD, the God of the heavens, has given me all the kingdoms of the earth and has appointed me to build him a temple at Jerusalem in Judah. Any of his people among you may go up, and may the LORD his God be with him.

◣ GOING DEEPER

JEREMIAH 25:1-7

The Seventy-Year Exile

[1] This is the word that came to Jeremiah concerning all the people of Judah in the fourth year of Jehoiakim son of Josiah, king of Judah (which was the first year of King Nebuchadnezzar of Babylon). [2] The prophet Jeremiah spoke concerning all the people of Judah and all the residents of Jerusalem as follows: [3] "From the thirteenth year of Josiah son of Amon, king of Judah, until this very day—twenty-three years—the word of the LORD has come to me, and I have spoken to you time and time again, but you have not obeyed. [4] The LORD sent all his servants the prophets to you time and time again, but you have not obeyed or even paid attention. [5] He announced, 'Turn, each of

you, from your evil way of life and from your evil deeds. Live in the land the Lᴏʀᴅ gave to you and your ancestors long ago and forever. ⁶ Do not follow other gods to serve them and to bow in worship to them, and do not anger me by the work of your hands. Then I will do you no harm.

⁷ "'But you have not obeyed me'—this is the Lᴏʀᴅ's declaration— 'with the result that you have angered me by the work of your hands and brought disaster on yourselves.'"

ROMANS 11:1–2

Israel's Rejection Not Total

¹ I ask, then, has God rejected his people? Absolutely not! For I too am an Israelite, a descendant of Abraham, from the tribe of Benjamin. ² God has not rejected his people whom he foreknew. Or don't you know what the Scripture says in the passage about Elijah—how he pleads with God against Israel?

Reflect

Second Chronicles ends with a retelling of the people's return from exile to start a new era of rebuilding and restoration (2Ch 36:22–23). The Chronicler recalls again this invitation to return from exile to reawaken their hope for spiritual renewal. Despite Israel's long time away from the land and their disobedient practices, God was still with them and He still had a purpose for His people.

Like Chronicles, Lent reminds us that God's promises are still true, even in the midst of our apathy, neglect, or outright disobedience.

Use this space to reflect on 1 & 2 Chronicles. Make notes on what broader themes about God and His people you've observed that are still relevant for you moving forward.

Let the whole earth sing to the LORD. Proclaim his salvation from day to day. Declare his glory among the nations, his wondrous works among all peoples.

1 CHRONICLES 16:23–24

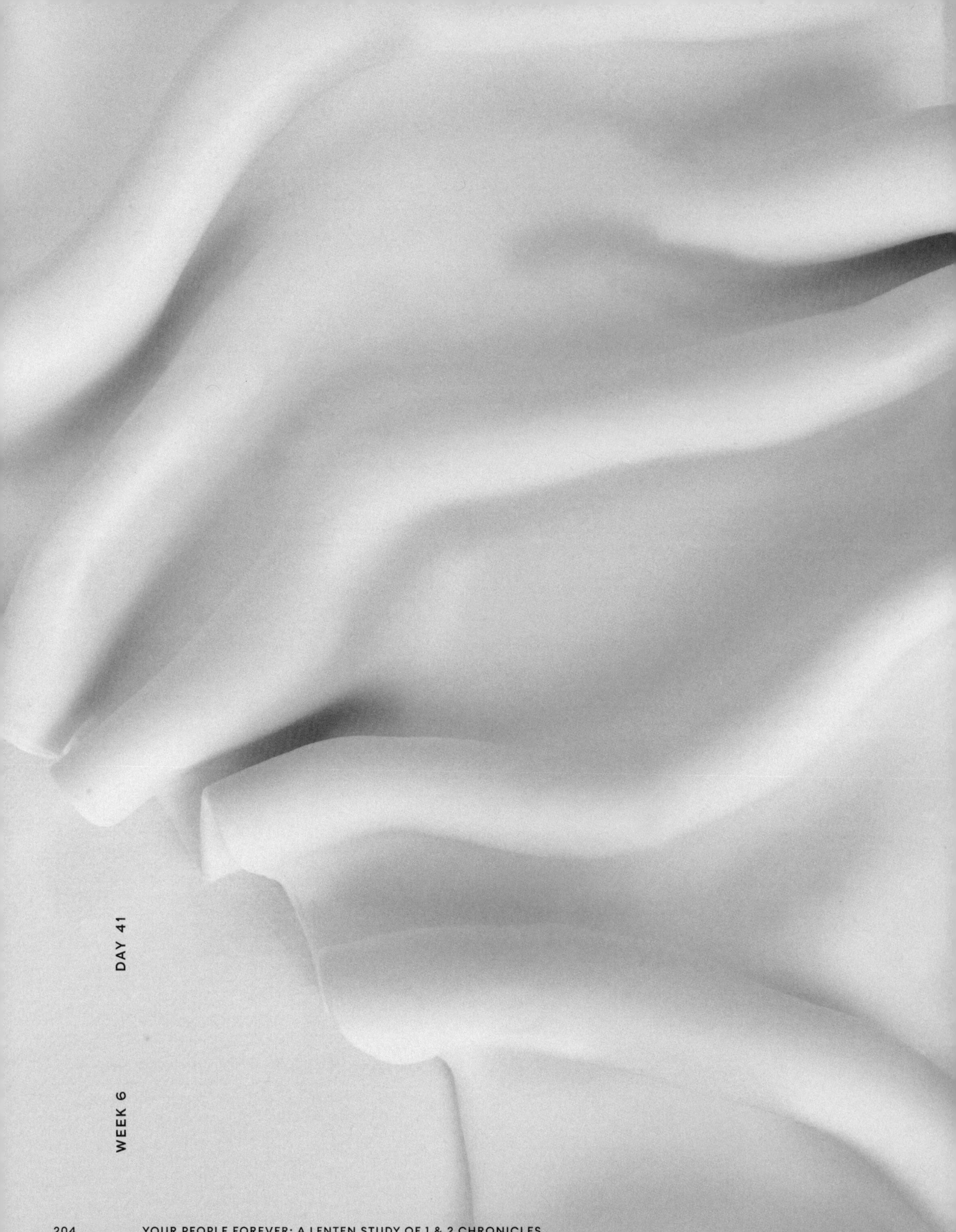

WEEK 6

DAY 41

Grace Day

Mankind, he has told each of you what is good and what it is the LORD requires of you: to act justly, to love faithfulness, and to walk humbly with your God.

Take this day to catch up on your reading, pray, and rest in the presence of the Lord.

MICAH 6:8

Holy Week

THE KING HAS COME

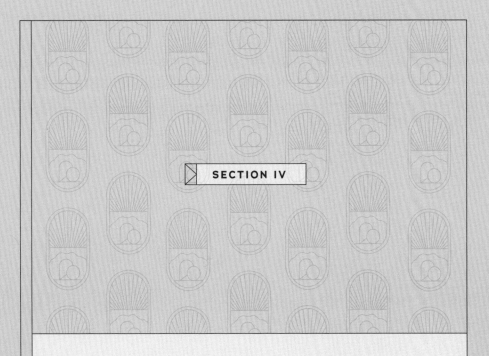

SECTION IV

As we make the turn into Holy Week, we remember the fullness of God's faithfulness that has been true every step of the journey. We lament the ways we have forgotten the truth of His promises, laying our burdens at the foot of the cross. As we read about Jesus's final days before His death and the ways He prepared His followers, we also join in a renewed hope for the future that He alone has secured.

Use this space to proclaim God's forever faithfulness and how it has shaped the way you enter Holy Week. Rejoice in the new life available to us in Christ as you prepare to celebrate Resurrection Sunday.

Prepare

Let the whole earth sing to the LORD. Proclaim his salvation from day to day. Declare his glory among the nations, his wondrous works among all peoples.

1 CHRONICLES 16:23–24

Palm Sunday

JOHN 12:12-50

The Triumphal Entry

¹² The next day, when the large crowd that had come to the festival heard that Jesus was coming to Jerusalem,

¹³ they took palm branches and went out to meet him.

They kept shouting:

"*Hosanna!*
Blessed is he who comes in the name of the Lord—the
    King of Israel!"

¹⁴ Jesus found a young donkey and sat on it, just as it is written:

¹⁵ Do not be afraid,
Daughter Zion. Look, your King is coming,
sitting on a donkey's colt.

¹⁶ His disciples did not understand these things at first. However, when Jesus was glorified, then they remembered that these things had been written about him and that they had done these things to him.

¹⁷ Meanwhile, the crowd, which had been with him when he called Lazarus out of the tomb and raised him from the dead, continued to testify. ¹⁸ This is also why the crowd met him, because they heard he had done this sign. ¹⁹ Then the Pharisees said to one another, "You see? You've accomplished nothing. Look, the world has gone after him!"

Jesus Predicts His Crucifixion

²⁰ Now some Greeks were among those who went up to worship at the festival. ²¹ So they came to Philip, who was from Bethsaida in Galilee, and requested of him, "Sir, we want to see Jesus." ²² Philip went and told Andrew; then Andrew and Philip went and told Jesus.

²³ Jesus replied to them, "The hour has come for the Son of Man to be glorified. ²⁴ Truly I tell you, unless a grain of wheat falls to the ground and dies, it remains by itself. But if it dies, it produces much fruit. ²⁵ The one who loves his life will lose it, and the one who hates his life in this world will keep it for eternal life. ²⁶ If anyone serves me, he must follow me. Where I am, there my servant also will be. If anyone serves me, the Father will honor him.

²⁷ "Now my soul is troubled. What should I say—Father, save me from this hour? But that is why I came to this hour. ²⁸ Father, glorify your name."

Then a voice came from heaven: "I have glorified it, and I will glorify it again."

²⁹ The crowd standing there heard it and said it was thunder. Others said, "An angel has spoken to him."

³⁰ Jesus responded, "This voice came, not for me, but for you. ³¹ Now is the judgment of this world. Now the ruler of this world will be cast out. ³² As for me, if I am lifted up from the earth I will draw all people to myself." ³³ He said this to indicate what kind of death he was about to die.

[34] Then the crowd replied to him, "We have heard from the law that the Messiah will remain forever. So how can you say, 'The Son of Man must be lifted up'? Who is this Son of Man?"

[35] Jesus answered, "The light will be with you only a little longer. Walk while you have the light so that darkness doesn't overtake you. The one who walks in darkness doesn't know where he's going. [36] While you have the light, believe in the light so that you may become children of light." Jesus said this, then went away and hid from them.

Isaiah's Prophecies Fulfilled

[37] Even though he had performed so many signs in their presence, they did not believe in him. [38] This was to fulfill the word of Isaiah the prophet, who said:

> Lord, who has believed our message?
> And to whom has the arm of the Lord been revealed?

[39] This is why they were unable to believe, because Isaiah also said:

> [40] He has blinded their eyes
> and hardened their hearts,
> so that they would not see with their eyes
> or understand with their hearts,
> and turn,
> and I would heal them.

[41] Isaiah said these things because he saw his glory and spoke about him.

[42] Nevertheless, many did believe in him even among the rulers, but because of the Pharisees they did not confess him, so that they would not be banned from the synagogue. [43] For they loved human praise more than praise from God.

A Summary of Jesus's Mission

[44] Jesus cried out, "The one who believes in me believes not in me, but in him who sent me. [45] And the one who sees me sees him who sent me. [46] I have come as light into the world, so that everyone who believes in me would not remain in darkness. [47] If anyone hears my words and doesn't keep them, I do not judge him; for I did not come to judge the world but to save the world. [48] The one who rejects me and doesn't receive my sayings has this as his judge: The word I have spoken will judge him on the last day. [49] For I have not spoken on my own, but the Father himself who sent me has given me a command to say everything

I have said. [50] I know that his command is eternal life. So the things that I speak, I speak just as the Father has told me."

GOING DEEPER

PSALM 118:25-29

[25] LORD, save us!

LORD, please grant us success!
[26] He who comes in the name
of the LORD is blessed.
From the house of the LORD we bless you.
[27] The LORD is God and has given us light.
Bind the festival sacrifice with cords
to the horns of the altar.
[28] You are my God, and I will give you thanks.
You are my God; I will exalt you.
[29] Give thanks to the LORD, for he is good;
his faithful love endures forever.

ZECHARIAH 9:9

Rejoice greatly, Daughter Zion!
Shout in triumph, Daughter Jerusalem!
Look, your King is coming to you;
he is righteous and victorious,
humble and riding on a donkey,
on a colt, the foal of a donkey.

Jesus Washes His Disciples' Feet

JOHN 13

Jesus Washes His Disciples' Feet

¹ Before the Passover Festival, Jesus knew that his hour had come to depart from this world to the Father. Having loved his own who were in the world, he loved them to the end.

² Now when it was time for supper, the devil had already put it into the heart of Judas, Simon Iscariot's son, to betray him. ³ Jesus knew that the Father had given everything into his hands, that he had come from God, and that he was going back to God. ⁴ So he got up from supper, laid aside his outer clothing, took a towel, and tied it around himself. ⁵ Next, he poured water into a basin and began to wash his disciples' feet and to dry them with the towel tied around him.

⁶ He came to Simon Peter, who asked him, "Lord, are you going to wash my feet?"

⁷ Jesus answered him, "What I'm doing you don't realize now, but afterward you will understand."

⁸ "You will never wash my feet," Peter said.

Jesus replied, "If I don't wash you, you have no part with me."

⁹ Simon Peter said to him, "Lord, not only my feet, but also my hands and my head."

¹⁰ "One who has bathed," Jesus told him, "doesn't need to wash anything except his feet, but he is completely clean. You are clean, but not all of you." ¹¹ For he knew who would betray him. This is why he said, "Not all of you are clean."

The Meaning of Foot Washing

¹² When Jesus had washed their feet and put on his outer clothing, he reclined again and said to them, "Do you know what I have done for you? ¹³ You call me Teacher and Lord—and you are speaking rightly, since that is what I am. ¹⁴ So if I, your Lord and Teacher, have washed your feet, you also ought to wash one another's feet. ¹⁵ For I have given you an example, that you also should do just as I have done for you.

¹⁶ "Truly I tell you, a servant is not greater than his master, and a messenger is not greater than the one who sent him. ¹⁷ If you know these things, you are blessed if you do them.

[18] "I'm not speaking about all of you; I know those I have chosen. But the Scripture must be fulfilled: The one who eats my bread has raised his heel against me. [19] I am telling you now before it happens, so that when it does happen you will believe that I am he. [20] Truly I tell you, whoever receives anyone I send receives me, and the one who receives me receives him who sent me."

Judas's Betrayal Predicted

[21] When Jesus had said this, he was troubled in his spirit and testified, "Truly I tell you, one of you will betray me."

[22] The disciples started looking at one another—uncertain which one he was speaking about. [23] One of his disciples, the one Jesus loved, was reclining close beside Jesus. [24] Simon Peter motioned to him to find out who it was he was talking about. [25] So he leaned back against Jesus and asked him, "Lord, who is it?"

[26] Jesus replied, "He's the one I give the piece of bread to after I have dipped it." When he had dipped the bread, he gave it to Judas, Simon Iscariot's son. [27] After Judas ate the piece of bread, Satan entered him. So Jesus told him, "What you're doing, do quickly."

[28] None of those reclining at the table knew why he said this to him. [29] Since Judas kept the money-bag, some thought that Jesus was telling him, "Buy what we need for the festival," or that he should give something to the poor. [30] After receiving the piece of bread, he immediately left. And it was night.

The New Command

[31] When he had left, Jesus said, "Now the Son of Man is glorified, and God is glorified in him. [32] If God is glorified in him, God will also glorify him in himself and will glorify him at once. [33] Little children, I am with you a little while longer. You will look for me, and just as I told the Jews, so now I tell you, 'Where I am going, you cannot come.'

[34] "I give you a new command: Love one another. Just as I have loved you, you are also to love one another. [35] By this everyone will know that you are my disciples, if you love one another."

Peter's Denials Predicted

36 "Lord," Simon Peter said to him, "where are you going?"

Jesus answered, "Where I am going you cannot follow me now, but you will follow later."

37 "Lord," Peter asked, "why can't I follow you now? I will lay down my life for you."

38 Jesus replied, "Will you lay down your life for me? Truly I tell you, a rooster will not crow until you have denied me three times."

NOTES

GOING DEEPER

PSALM 51:6–7

6 Surely you desire integrity in the inner self,
and you teach me wisdom deep within.
7 Purify me with hyssop, and I will be clean;
wash me, and I will be whiter than snow.

Jesus Promises His Presence

JOHN 14

The Way to the Father

¹ "Don't let your heart be troubled. Believe in God; believe also in me. ² In my Father's house are many rooms. If it were not so, would I have told you that I am going to prepare a place for you? ³ If I go away and prepare a place for you, I will come again and take you to myself, so that where I am you may be also. ⁴ You know the way to where I am going."

⁵ "Lord," Thomas said, "we don't know where you're going. How can we know the way?"

⁶ Jesus told him, "I am the way, the truth, and the life. No one comes to the Father except through me. ⁷ If you know me, you will also know my Father. From now on you do know him and have seen him."

Jesus Reveals the Father

⁸ "Lord," said Philip, "show us the Father, and that's enough for us."

⁹ Jesus said to him, "Have I been among you all this time and you do not know me, Philip? The one who has seen me has seen the Father. How can you say, 'Show us the Father'? ¹⁰ Don't you believe that I am in the Father and the Father is in me? The words I speak to you I do not speak on my own. The Father who lives in me does his works. ¹¹ Believe me that I am in the Father and the Father is in me. Otherwise, believe because of the works themselves.

Praying in Jesus's Name

[12] "Truly I tell you, the one who believes in me will also do the works that I do. And he will do even greater works than these, because I am going to the Father. [13] Whatever you ask in my name, I will do it so that the Father may be glorified in the Son. [14] If you ask me anything in my name, I will do it.

Another Counselor Promised

[15] "If you love me, you will keep my commands. [16] And I will ask the Father, and he will give you another Counselor to be with you forever. [17] He is the Spirit of truth. The world is unable to receive him because it doesn't see him or know him. But you do know him, because he remains with you and will be in you.

The Father, the Son, and the Holy Spirit

[18] "I will not leave you as orphans; I am coming to you.

[19] In a little while the world will no longer see me, but you will see me. Because I live, you will live too. [20] On that day you will know that I am in my Father, you are in me, and I am in you. [21] The one who has my commands and keeps them is the one who loves me. And the one who loves me will be loved by my Father. I also will love him and will reveal myself to him."

[22] Judas (not Iscariot) said to him, "Lord, how is it you're going to reveal yourself to us and not to the world?"

[23] Jesus answered, "If anyone loves me, he will keep my word. My Father will love him, and we will come to him and make our home with him. [24] The one who doesn't love me will not keep my words. The word that you hear is not mine but is from the Father who sent me.

[25] "I have spoken these things to you while I remain with you. [26] But the Counselor, the Holy Spirit, whom the Father will send in my name, will teach you all things and remind you of everything I have told you.

Jesus's Gift of Peace

[27] "Peace I leave with you. My peace I give to you. I do not give to you as the world gives. Don't let your heart be troubled or fearful. [28] You have heard me tell you, 'I am going away and I am coming to you.' If you loved me, you would rejoice that I am going to the Father, because the Father is greater than I. [29] I have told you now before it happens so that when it does happen you may believe. [30] I will not talk with you much longer, because the ruler of the world is coming. He has no power over me. [31] On the contrary, so that the world may know that I love the Father, I do as the Father commanded me.

"Get up; let's leave this place."

JOHN 15:1–25

The Vine and the Branches

[1] "I am the true vine, and my Father is the gardener. [2] Every branch in me that does not produce fruit he removes, and he prunes every branch that produces fruit so that it will produce more fruit. [3] You are already clean because of the word I have spoken to you. [4] Remain in me, and I in you. Just as a branch is unable to produce fruit by itself unless it remains on the vine, neither can you unless you remain in me. [5] I am the vine; you are the branches. The one who remains in me and I in him produces much fruit, because you can do nothing without me. [6] If anyone does not remain in me, he is thrown aside like a branch and he withers. They gather them, throw them into the fire, and they are burned. [7] If you remain in me and my words remain in you, ask whatever you want and it will be done for you. [8] My Father is glorified by this: that you produce much fruit and prove to be my disciples.

Christlike Love

[9] "As the Father has loved me, I have also loved you. Remain in my love. [10] If you keep my commands you will remain in my love, just as I have kept my Father's commands and remain in his love.

[11] "I have told you these things so that my joy may be in you and your joy may be complete.

[12] "This is my command: Love one another as I have loved you. [13] No one has greater love than this: to lay down his life for his friends. [14] You are my friends if you do what I command you. [15] I do not call you servants anymore, because a servant doesn't know what his master is doing. I have called you friends, because I have made known to you everything I have heard from my Father. [16] You did not choose me, but I chose you. I appointed you to go and produce fruit and that your fruit should remain, so that whatever you ask the Father in my name, he will give you.

[17] "This is what I command you: Love one another.

Persecutions Predicted

[18] "If the world hates you, understand that it hated me before it hated you. [19] If you were of the world, the world would love you as its own. However, because you are not of the world, but I have chosen you out of it, the world hates you. [20] Remember the word I spoke to you: 'A servant is not greater than his master.' If they persecuted me, they will also persecute you. If they kept my word, they will also keep yours. [21] But they will do all these things to you on account of my name, because they don't know the one who sent me. [22] If I had not come and spoken to them, they would not be guilty of sin. Now they have no excuse for their sin. [23] The one who hates me also hates my Father. [24] If I had not done the works among them that no one else has done, they would not be guilty of sin. Now they have seen and hated both me and my Father. [25] But this happened so that the statement written in their law might be fulfilled: They hated me for no reason."

◥ GOING DEEPER

ISAIAH 42:16

"I will lead the blind by a way they did not know;
I will guide them on paths they have not known.
I will turn darkness to light in front of them
and rough places into level ground.
This is what I will do for them,
and I will not abandon them."

The Promised Counselor

26 "When the Counselor comes, the one I will send to you from the Father —the Spirit of truth who proceeds from the Father—he will testify about me. 27 You also will testify, because you have been with me from the beginning."

JOHN 16

1 "I have told you these things to keep you from stumbling. 2 They will ban you from the synagogues. In fact, a time is coming when anyone who kills you will think he is offering service to God. 3 They will do these things because they haven't known the Father or me. 4 But I have told you these things so that when their time comes you will remember I told them to you. I didn't tell you these things from the beginning, because I was with you. 5 But now I am going away to him who sent me, and not one of you asks me, 'Where are you going?' 6 Yet, because I have spoken these things to you, sorrow has filled your heart. 7 Nevertheless, I am telling you the truth.

It is for your benefit that I go away, because if I don't go away the Counselor will not come to you.

If I go, I will send him to you. 8 When he comes, he will convict the world about sin, righteousness, and judgment: 9 About sin, because they do not believe in me; 10 about righteousness, because I am going to the Father and you will no longer see me; 11 and about judgment, because the ruler of this world has been judged.

12 "I still have many things to tell you, but you can't bear them now. 13 When the Spirit of truth comes, he will guide you into all the truth. For he will not speak on his own, but he will speak whatever he hears. He will also declare to you what is to come. 14 He will glorify me, because he will take from what is mine and declare it to you. 15 Everything the Father has is mine. This is why I told you that he takes from what is mine and will declare it to you.

Sorrow Turned to Joy

[16] "In a little while, you will no longer see me; again in a little while, you will see me."

[17] Then some of his disciples said to one another, "What is this he's telling us: 'In a little while, you will not see me; again in a little while, you will see me,' and, 'Because I am going to the Father'?" [18] They said, "What is this he is saying, 'In a little while'? We don't know what he's talking about."

[19] Jesus knew they wanted to ask him, and so he said to them, "Are you asking one another about what I said, 'In a little while, you will not see me; again in a little while, you will see me'? [20] Truly I tell you, you will weep and mourn, but the world will rejoice. You will become sorrowful, but your sorrow will turn to joy. [21] When a woman is in labor, she has pain because her time has come. But when she has given birth to a child, she no longer remembers the suffering because of the joy that a person has been born into the world. [22] So you also have sorrow now. But I will see you again. Your hearts will rejoice, and no one will take away your joy from you.

[23] "In that day you will not ask me anything. Truly I tell you, anything you ask the Father in my name, he will give you. [24] Until now you have asked for nothing in my name. Ask and you will receive, so that your joy may be complete.

Jesus the Victor

[25] "I have spoken these things to you in figures of speech. A time is coming when I will no longer speak to you in figures, but I will tell you plainly about the Father. [26] On that day you will ask in my name, and I am not telling you that I will ask the Father on your behalf. [27] For the Father himself loves you, because you have loved me and have believed that I came from God. [28] I came from the Father and have come into the world. Again, I am leaving the world and going to the Father."

[29] His disciples said, "Look, now you're speaking plainly and not using any figurative language. [30] Now we know that you know everything and don't need anyone to question you. By this we believe that you came from God."

³¹ Jesus responded to them, "Do you now believe? ³² Indeed, an hour is coming, and has come, when each of you will be scattered to his own home, and you will leave me alone. Yet I am not alone, because the Father is with me. ³³ I have told you these things so that in me you may have peace. You will have suffering in this world. Be courageous! I have conquered the world."

⬛ GOING DEEPER

JOEL 2:28-29

God's Promise of His Spirit

²⁸ "After this

I will pour out my Spirit on
all humanity;

then your sons and your daughters will prophesy,
your old men will have dreams,
and your young men will see visions.
²⁹ I will even pour out my Spirit
on the male and female slaves in those days."

Jesus Prays for His Disciples

WEEK 7   DAY 46

JOHN 17

Jesus Prays for Himself

¹ Jesus spoke these things, looked up to heaven, and said, "Father, the hour has come. Glorify your Son so that the Son may glorify you, ² since you gave him authority over all people, so that he may give eternal life to everyone you have given him. ³ This is eternal life: that they may know you, the only true God, and the one you have sent —Jesus Christ. ⁴ I have glorified you on the earth by completing the work you gave me to do. ⁵ Now, Father, glorify me in your presence with that glory I had with you before the world existed.

Jesus Prays for His Disciples

⁶ "I have revealed your name to the people you gave me from the world. They were yours, you gave them to me, and they have kept your word. ⁷ Now they know that everything you have given me is from you, ⁸ because I have given them the words you gave me. They have received them and have known for certain that I came from you. They have believed that you sent me.

9 "I pray for them. I am not praying for the world but for those you have given me, because they are yours. 10 Everything I have is yours, and everything you have is mine, and I am glorified in them. 11 I am no longer in the world, but they are in the world, and I am coming to you. Holy Father, protect them by your name that you have given me, so that they may be one as we are one. 12 While I was with them, I was protecting them by your name that you have given me. I guarded them and not one of them is lost, except the son of destruction, so that the Scripture may be fulfilled. 13 Now I am coming to you, and I speak these things in the world so that they may have my joy completed in them. 14 I have given them your word. The world hated them because they are not of the world, just as I am not of the world. 15 I am not praying that you take them out of the world but that you protect them from the evil one. 16 They are not of the world, just as I am not of the world. 17 Sanctify them by the truth; your word is truth. 18 As you sent me into the world, I also have sent them into the world. 19 I sanctify myself for them, so that they also may be sanctified by the truth.

Jesus Prays for All Believers

20 "I pray not only for these, but also for those who believe in me through their word. 21 May they all be one, as you, Father, are in me and I am in you. May they also be in us, so that the world may believe you sent me. 22 I have given them the glory you have given me, so that they may be one as we are one. 23 I am in them and you are in me, so that they may be made completely one, that the world may know you have sent me and have loved them as you have loved me.

24 "Father, I want those you have given me to be with me where I am, so that they will see my glory, which you have given me because you loved me before the world's foundation.

25 Righteous Father, the world has not known you. However, I have known you, and they have known that you sent me. 26 I made your name known to them and will continue to make it known, so that the love you have loved me with may be in them and I may be in them."

JOHN 18:1-27

Jesus Betrayed

1 After Jesus had said these things, he went out with his disciples across the Kidron Valley, where there was a garden, and he and his disciples went into it. 2 Judas, who betrayed him, also knew the place, because Jesus often met there with his disciples. 3 So Judas took a company of soldiers and some officials from the chief priests and the Pharisees and came there with lanterns, torches, and weapons.

4 Then Jesus, knowing everything that was about to happen to him, went out and said to them, "Who is it that you're seeking?"

5 "Jesus of Nazareth," they answered.

"I am he," Jesus told them.

Judas, who betrayed him, was also standing with them. [6] When Jesus told them, "I am he," they stepped back and fell to the ground.

[7] Then he asked them again, "Who is it that you're seeking?"

"Jesus of Nazareth," they said.

[8] "I told you I am he," Jesus replied. "So if you're looking for me, let these men go." [9] This was to fulfill the words he had said: "I have not lost one of those you have given me."

[10] Then Simon Peter, who had a sword, drew it, struck the high priest's servant, and cut off his right ear. (The servant's name was Malchus.)

[11] At that, Jesus said to Peter, "Put your sword away! Am I not to drink the cup the Father has given me?"

Jesus Arrested and Taken to Annas

[12] Then the company of soldiers, the commander, and the Jewish officials arrested Jesus and tied him up. [13] First they led him to Annas, since he was the father-in-law of Caiaphas, who was high priest that year. [14] Caiaphas was theone who had advised the Jews that it would be better for one man to die for the people.

Peter Denies Jesus

[15] Simon Peter was following Jesus, as was another disciple. That disciple was an acquaintance of the high priest; so he went with Jesus into the high priest's courtyard. [16] But Peter remained standing outside by the door. So the other disciple, the one known to the high priest, went out and spoke to the girl who was the doorkeeper and brought Peter in.

[17] Then the servant girl who was the doorkeeper said to Peter, "You aren't one of this man's disciples too, are you?"

"I am not," he said. [18] Now the servants and the officials had made a charcoal fire, because it was cold. They were standing there warming themselves, and Peter was standing with them, warming himself.

Jesus Before Annas

[19] The high priest questioned Jesus about his disciples and about his teaching.

[20] "I have spoken openly to the world," Jesus answered him. "I have always taught in the synagogue and in the temple, where all the Jews gather, and I

haven't spoken anything in secret. ²¹ Why do you question me? Question those who heard what I told them. Look, they know what I said."

²² When he had said these things, one of the officials standing by slapped Jesus, saying, "Is this the way you answer the high priest?"

²³ "If I have spoken wrongly," Jesus answered him, "give evidence about the wrong; but if rightly, why do you hit me?" ²⁴ Then Annas sent him bound to Caiaphas the high priest.

Peter Denies Jesus Twice More

²⁵ Now Simon Peter was standing and warming himself. They said to him, "You aren't one of his disciples too, are you?"

He denied it and said, "I am not."

²⁶ One of the high priest's servants, a relative of the man whose ear Peter had cut off, said, "Didn't I see you with him in the garden?" ²⁷ Peter denied it again. Immediately a rooster crowed.

⬛ GOING DEEPER

JUDE 24–25

²⁴ Now to him who is able to protect you from stumbling and to make you stand in the presence of his glory, without blemish and with great joy, ²⁵ to the only God our Savior, through Jesus Christ our Lord, be glory, majesty, power, and authority before all time, now and forever. Amen.

Good Friday

JOHN 18:28-40

Jesus Before Pilate

[28] Then they led Jesus from Caiaphas to the governor's headquarters. It was early morning. They did not enter the headquarters themselves; otherwise they would be defiled and unable to eat the Passover.

[29] So Pilate came out to them and said, "What charge do you bring against this man?"

[30] They answered him, "If this man weren't a criminal, we wouldn't have handed him over to you."

[31] Pilate told them, "You take him and judge him according to your law."

"It's not legal for us to put anyone to death," the Jews declared. [32] They said this so that Jesus's words might be fulfilled indicating what kind of death he was going to die.

[33] Then Pilate went back into the headquarters, summoned Jesus, and said to him, "Are you the king of the Jews?"

[34] Jesus answered, "Are you asking this on your own, or have others told you about me?"

[35] "I'm not a Jew, am I?" Pilate replied. "Your own nation and the chief priests handed you over to me. What have you done?"

[36] "My kingdom is not of this world," said Jesus. "If my kingdom were of this world, my servants would fight, so that I wouldn't be handed over to the Jews. But as it is, my kingdom is not from here."

[37] "You are a king then?" Pilate asked.

"You say that I'm a king," Jesus replied. "I was born for this, and I have come into the world for this: to testify to the truth. Everyone who is of the truth listens to my voice."

[38] "What is truth?" said Pilate.

Jesus or Barabbas

After he had said this, he went out to the Jews again and told them, "I find no grounds for charging him. [39] You have a custom that I release one prisoner to you at the Passover. So, do you want me to release to you the king of the Jews?"

[40] They shouted back, "Not this man, but Barabbas!" Now Barabbas was a revolutionary.

JOHN 19

Jesus Flogged and Mocked

[1] Then Pilate took Jesus and had him flogged. [2] The soldiers also twisted together a crown of thorns, put it on his head, and clothed him in a purple robe. [3] And they kept coming up to him and saying, "Hail, king of the Jews!" and were slapping his face.

[4] Pilate went outside again and said to them, "Look, I'm bringing him out to you to let you know I find no grounds for charging him." [5] Then Jesus came out wearing the crown of thorns and the purple robe. Pilate said to them, "Here is the man!"

Pilate Sentences Jesus to Death

⁶ When the chief priests and the temple servants saw him, they shouted, "Crucify! Crucify!"

Pilate responded, "Take him and crucify him yourselves, since I find no grounds for charging him."

⁷ "We have a law," the Jews replied to him, "and according to that law he ought to die, because he made himself the Son of God."

⁸ When Pilate heard this statement, he was more afraid than ever. ⁹ He went back into the headquarters and asked Jesus, "Where are you from?" But Jesus did not give him an answer. ¹⁰ So Pilate said to him, "Do you refuse to speak to me? Don't you know that I have the authority to release you and the authority to crucify you?"

¹¹ "You would have no authority over me at all," Jesus answered him, "if it hadn't been given you from above. This is why the one who handed me over to you has the greater sin."

¹² From that moment Pilate kept trying to release him. But the Jews shouted, "If you release this man, you are not Caesar's friend. Anyone who makes himself a king opposes Caesar!"

¹³ When Pilate heard these words, he brought Jesus outside. He sat down on the judge's seat in a place called the Stone Pavement (but in Aramaic, *Gabbatha*). ¹⁴ It was the preparation day for the Passover, and it was about noon. Then he told the Jews, "Here is your king!"

¹⁵ They shouted, "Take him away! Take him away! Crucify him!"

Pilate said to them, "Should I crucify your king?"

"We have no king but Caesar!" the chief priests answered.

¹⁶ Then he handed him over to be crucified.

The Crucifixion

Then they took Jesus away. ¹⁷ Carrying the cross by himself, he went out to what is called Place of the Skull, which in Aramaic is called *Golgotha*. ¹⁸ There they crucified him and two others with him, one on either side, with Jesus in the middle. ¹⁹ Pilate also had a sign made and put on the cross. It said: JESUS OF NAZARETH, THE KING OF THE JEWS ²⁰ Many of the Jews read this sign, because the place where Jesus was crucified was near the city, and it was written in Aramaic, Latin, and Greek. ²¹ So the chief priests of the Jews said to Pilate, "Don't write, 'The king of the Jews,' but that he said, 'I am the king of the Jews.'"

²² Pilate replied, "What I have written, I have written."

²³ When the soldiers crucified Jesus, they took his clothes and divided them into four parts, a part for each soldier. They also took the tunic, which was seamless, woven in one piece from the top. ²⁴ So they said to one another, "Let's not tear it, but cast lots for it, to see who gets it." This happened that the Scripture might be fulfilled that says: They divided my clothes among themselves, and they cast lots for my clothing. This is what the soldiers did.

Jesus's Provision for His Mother

²⁵ Standing by the cross of Jesus were his mother, his mother's sister, Mary the wife of Clopas, and Mary Magdalene. ²⁶ When Jesus saw his mother and the disciple he loved standing there, he said to his mother, "Woman, here is your son." ²⁷ Then he said to the disciple, "Here is your mother." And from that hour the disciple took her into his home.

The Finished Work of Jesus

²⁸ After this, when Jesus knew that everything was now finished that the Scripture might be fulfilled, he said, "I'm thirsty." ²⁹ A jar full of sour wine was sitting there; so they fixed a sponge full of sour wine on a hyssop branch and held it up to his mouth.

³⁰ When Jesus had received the sour wine, he said, "It is finished."

Then bowing his head, he gave up his spirit.

Jesus's Side Pierced

31 Since it was the preparation day, the Jews did not want the bodies to remain on the cross on the Sabbath (for that Sabbath was a special day). They requested that Pilate have the men's legs broken and that their bodies be taken away. 32 So the soldiers came and broke the legs of the first man and of the other one who had been crucified with him. 33 When they came to Jesus, they did not break his legs since they saw that he was already dead. 34 But one of the soldiers pierced his side with a spear, and at once blood and water came out. 35 He who saw this has testified so that you also may believe. His testimony is true, and he knows he is telling the truth. 36 For these things happened so that the Scripture would be fulfilled: Not one of his bones will be broken. 37 Also, another Scripture says: They will look at the one they pierced.

Jesus's Burial

38 After this, Joseph of Arimathea, who was a disciple of Jesus—but secretly because of his fear of the Jews—asked Pilate that he might remove Jesus's body. Pilate gave him permission; so he came and took his body away. 39 Nicodemus (who had previously come to him at night) also came, bringing a mixture of about seventy-five pounds of myrrh and aloes. 40 They took Jesus's body and wrapped it in linen cloths with the fragrant spices, according to the burial custom of the Jews. 41 There was a garden in the place where he was crucified. A new tomb was in the garden; no one had yet been placed in it. 42 They placed Jesus there because of the Jewish day of preparation and since the tomb was nearby.

◗ GOING DEEPER

ISAIAH 52:13-15

The Servant's Suffering and Exaltation

13 See, my servant will be successful;
he will be raised and lifted up and greatly exalted.

14 Just as many were appalled at you—
his appearance was so disfigured
that he did not look like a man,
and his form did not resemble a human being—
15 so he will sprinkle many nations.
Kings will shut their mouths because of him,
for they will see what had not been told them,
and they will understand what they had not heard.

ISAIAH 53:1-7

1 Who has believed what we have heard?
And to whom has the arm of the LORD been revealed?
2 He grew up before him like a young plant
and like a root out of dry ground.
He didn't have an impressive form
or majesty that we should look at him,
no appearance that we should desire him.
3 He was despised and rejected by men,
a man of suffering who knew what sickness was.
He was like someone people turned away from;
he was despised, and we didn't value him.

4 Yet he himself bore our sicknesses,
and he carried our pains;
but we in turn regarded him stricken,
struck down by God, and afflicted.
5 But he was pierced because of our rebellion,
crushed because of our iniquities;
punishment for our peace was on him,
and we are healed by his wounds.
6 We all went astray like sheep;
we all have turned to our own way;
and the LORD has punished him
for the iniquity of us all.

7 He was oppressed and afflicted,
yet he did not open his mouth.
Like a lamb led to the slaughter
and like a sheep silent before her shearers,
he did not open his mouth.

Holy
Saturday

MATTHEW 27:62-66

The Closely Guarded Tomb

⁶² The next day, which followed the preparation day, the chief priests and the Pharisees gathered before Pilate ⁶³ and said, "Sir, we remember that while this deceiver was still alive he said,

'After three days I will rise again.'

⁶⁴ So give orders that the tomb be made secure until the third day. Otherwise, his disciples may come, steal him, and tell the people, 'He has been raised from the dead,' and the last deception will be worse than the first."

⁶⁵ "Take guards," Pilate told them. "Go and make it as secure as you know how." ⁶⁶ They went and secured the tomb by setting a seal on the stone and placing the guards.

LUKE 23:54-56

⁵⁴ It was the preparation day, and the Sabbath was about to begin. ⁵⁵ The women who had come with him from Galilee followed along and observed the tomb and how his body was placed. ⁵⁶ Then they returned and prepared spices and perfumes. And they rested on the Sabbath according to the commandment.

🔖 GOING DEEPER

ISAIAH 53:8-12

⁸ He was taken away because of oppression and judgment,
and who considered his fate?
For he was cut off from the land of the living;
he was struck because of my people's rebellion.
⁹ He was assigned a grave with the wicked,
but he was with a rich man at his death,
because he had done no violence
and had not spoken deceitfully.

¹⁰ Yet the LORD was pleased to crush him severely.
When you make him a guilt offering,
he will see his seed, he will prolong his days,
and by his hand, the LORD's pleasure will be accomplished.
¹¹ After his anguish,
he will see light and be satisfied.
By his knowledge,
my righteous servant will justify many,
and he will carry their iniquities.
¹² Therefore I will give him the many as a portion,
and he will receive the mighty as spoil,
because he willingly submitted to death,
and was counted among the rebels;
yet he bore the sin of many
and interceded for the rebels.

Easter Sunday

JOHN 20:1–10

The Empty Tomb

¹ On the first day of the week Mary Magdalene came to the tomb early, while it was still dark. She saw that the stone had been removed from the tomb. ² So she went running to Simon Peter and to the other disciple, the one Jesus loved, and said to them, "They've taken the Lord out of the tomb, and we don't know where they've put him!"

³ At that, Peter and the other disciple went out, heading for the tomb. ⁴ The two were running together, but the other disciple outran Peter and got to the tomb first. ⁵ Stooping down, he saw the linen cloths lying there, but he did not go in. ⁶ Then, following him, Simon Peter also came. He entered the tomb and saw the linen cloths lying there. ⁷ The wrapping that had been on his head was not lying with the linen cloths but was folded up in a separate place by itself. ⁸ The other disciple, who had reached the tomb first, then also went in, saw, and believed. ⁹ For they did not yet understand the Scripture that he must rise from the dead. ¹⁰ Then the disciples returned to the place where they were staying.

LUKE 24:1-12

Resurrection Morning

1 On the first day of the week, very early in the morning, they came to the tomb, bringing the spices they had prepared. 2 They found the stone rolled away from the tomb. 3 They went in but did not find the body of the Lord Jesus. 4 While they were perplexed about this, suddenly two men stood by them in dazzling clothes. 5 So the women were terrified and bowed down to the ground.

"Why are you looking for the living among the dead?" asked the men. 6 "He is not here, but he has risen! Remember how he spoke to you when he was still in Galilee, 7 saying, 'It is necessary that the Son of Man be betrayed into the hands of sinful men, be crucified, and rise on the third day'?" 8 And they remembered his words.

9 Returning from the tomb, they reported all these things to the Eleven and to all the rest. 10 Mary Magdalene, Joanna, Mary the mother of James, and the other women with them were telling the apostles these things. 11 But these words seemed like nonsense to them, and they did not believe the women. 12 Peter, however, got up and ran to the tomb. When he stooped to look in, he saw only the linen cloths. So he went away, amazed at what had happened.

◼ GOING DEEPER

PSALM 16:9-11

9 Therefore my heart is glad
and my whole being rejoices;

my body also rests securely.
10 For you will not abandon me to Sheol;
you will not allow your faithful one to see decay.
11 You reveal the path of life to me;
in your presence is abundant joy;
at your right hand are eternal pleasures.

BENEDICTION

Lord, there is no one like you, and
there is no God besides you, as all
we have heard confirms. And who
is like your people Israel? God,
you came to one nation on earth
to redeem a people for yourself,
to make a name for yourself
through great and awesome works
by driving out nations before your
people you redeemed from Egypt.
You made your people Israel your
own people forever, and you,
Lord, have become their God.

1 CHRONICLES 17:20-22

Tips for Memorizing Scripture

At She Reads Truth, we believe Scripture memorization is an important discipline in your walk with God. Committing God's Truth to memory means He can minister to us—and we can minister to others—through His Word no matter where we are. As you approach the Weekly Truth passage in this book, try these memorization tips to see which techniques work best for you!

STUDY IT

Study the passage in its biblical context and ask yourself a few questions before you begin to memorize it: What does this passage say? What does it mean? How would I say this in my own words? What does it teach me about God? Understanding what the passage means helps you know why it is important to carry it with you wherever you go.

Break the passage into smaller sections, memorizing a phrase at a time.

PRAY IT

Use the passage you are memorizing as a prompt for prayer.

WRITE IT

Dedicate a notebook to Scripture memorization and write the passage over and over again.

Diagram the passage after you write it out. Place a square around the verbs, underline the nouns, and circle any adjectives or adverbs. Say the passage aloud several times, emphasizing the verbs as you repeat it. Then do the same thing again with the nouns, then the adjectives and adverbs.

Write out the first letter of each word in the passage somewhere you can reference it throughout the week as you work on your memorization.

Use a whiteboard to write out the passage. Erase a few words at a time as you continue to repeat it aloud. Keep erasing parts of the passage until you have it all committed to memory.

CREATE

If you can, make up a tune for the passage to sing as you go about your day, or try singing it to the tune of a favorite song.

Sketch the passage, visualizing what each phrase would look like in the form of a picture. Or, try using calligraphy or altering the style of your handwriting as you write it out.

Use hand signals or signs to come up with associations for each word or phrase and repeat the movements as you practice.

SAY IT

Repeat the passage out loud to yourself as you are going through the rhythm of your day—getting ready, pouring your coffee, waiting in traffic, or making dinner.

Listen to the passage read aloud to you.

Record a voice memo on your phone and listen to it throughout the day or play it on an audio Bible.

SHARE IT

Memorize the passage with a friend, family member, or mentor. Spontaneously challenge each other to recite the passage, or pick a time to review your passage and practice saying it from memory together.

Send the passage as an encouraging text to a friend, testing yourself as you type to see how much you have memorized so far.

KEEP AT IT!

Set reminders on your phone to prompt you to practice your passage.

Purchase a She Reads Truth 12 Card Set or keep a stack of note cards with Scripture you are memorizing by your bed. Practice reciting what you've memorized previously before you go to sleep, ending with the passages you are currently learning. If you wake up in the middle of the night, review them again instead of grabbing your phone. Read them out loud before you get out of bed in the morning.

CSB BOOK ABBREVIATIONS

OLD TESTAMENT

GN Genesis	**JB** Job	**HAB** Habakkuk	**PHP** Philippians
EX Exodus	**PS** Psalms	**ZPH** Zephaniah	**COL** Colossians
LV Leviticus	**PR** Proverbs	**HG** Haggai	**1TH** 1 Thessalonians
NM Numbers	**EC** Ecclesiastes	**ZCH** Zechariah	**2TH** 2 Thessalonians
DT Deuteronomy	**SG** Song of Solomon	**MAL** Malachi	**1TM** 1 Timothy
JOS Joshua	**IS** Isaiah		**2TM** 2 Timothy
JDG Judges	**JR** Jeremiah	### NEW TESTAMENT	**TI** Titus
RU Ruth	**LM** Lamentations	**MT** Matthew	**PHM** Philemon
1SM 1 Samuel	**EZK** Ezekiel	**MK** Mark	**HEB** Hebrews
2SM 2 Samuel	**DN** Daniel	**LK** Luke	**JMS** James
1KG 1 Kings	**HS** Hosea	**JN** John	**1PT** 1 Peter
2KG 2 Kings	**JL** Joel	**AC** Acts	**2PT** 2 Peter
1CH 1 Chronicles	**AM** Amos	**RM** Romans	**1JN** 1 John
2CH 2 Chronicles	**OB** Obadiah	**1CO** 1 Corinthians	**2JN** 2 John
EZR Ezra	**JNH** Jonah	**2CO** 2 Corinthians	**3JN** 3 John
NEH Nehemiah	**MC** Micah	**GL** Galatians	**JD** Jude
EST Esther	**NAH** Nahum	**EPH** Ephesians	**RV** Revelation

BIBLIOGRAPHY

Crocker, Lacy K. "Temple, Solomon's." In *The Lexham Bible Dictionary*, edited by John D. Barry, David Bomar, Derek R. Brown, Rachel Klippenstein, Douglas Mangum, Carrie Sinclair Wolcott, Lazarus Wentz, Elliot Ritzema, and Wendy Widder. Bellingham: Lexham Press, 2016.

House, Paul R. *Old Testament Theology*. Downers Grove: InterVarsity Press, 1998.

Japhet, Sara. *I & II Chronicles*. Louisville: Westminster John Knox Press, 1993.

Mandell, Sara. "Hebrews." In *Eerdmans Dictionary of the Bible*, edited by David Noel Freedman, Allen C. Myers, and Astrid B. Beck. Grand Rapids: W.B. Eerdmans, 2000.

Mason, Eric F. "Judea." In *Eerdmans Dictionary of the Bible*, edited by David Noel Freedman, Allen C. Myers, and Astrid B. Beck. Grand Rapids: W.B. Eerdmans, 2000.

Matheney, M. Pierce. "Temple of Jerusalem." In *Holman Illustrated Bible Dictionary*, edited by Chad Brand, Charles Draper, Archie England, Steve Bond, E. Ray Clendenen, and Trent C. Butler. Nashville: Holman Bible Publishers, 2003.

Meyers, Carol. "Temple, Jerusalem." In *The Anchor Yale Bible Dictionary*, edited by David Noel Freedman. New York: Doubleday, 1992.

Spurgeon, C. H. *Morning and Evening: Daily Readings*. London: Passmore & Alabaster, 1896.

Thompson, J. A. *1, 2 Chronicles*. Vol. 9. The New American Commentary. Nashville: Broadman & Holman Publishers, 1994.

LOOKING FOR DEVOTIONALS?

Download the **She Reads Truth app** to find devotionals that complement your daily Scripture reading. If you're stuck on a passage, hop into the community discussion to connect with other Shes who are reading God's Word right along with you.

You just spent 49 days in the Word of God!

MY FAVORITE DAY OF THIS READING PLAN:

ONE THING I LEARNED ABOUT GOD:

WHAT WAS GOD DOING IN MY LIFE DURING THIS STUDY?

HOW DID I FIND DELIGHT IN GOD'S WORD?

WHAT DID I LEARN THAT I WANT TO SHARE WITH SOMEONE ELSE?

A SPECIFIC SCRIPTURE THAT ENCOURAGED ME:

A SPECIFIC SCRIPTURE THAT CHALLENGED AND CONVICTED ME: